Building an Empire -
Failing our way to millions

By Steven Rozenberg

ISBN: 9781095026731
ISBN-13:

DEDICATION

This book is dedicated to my wife Renee and son Jett. You are the reason I work as hard as I do. Thanks for pushing me beyond my limits, and for being the spirit that drives me.

Contents

Chapter 3..49

Creating the Empire Brand...................49

ACKNOWLEDGMENTS

I'd like to acknowledge the following people, without whom this book would never have been possible:

My mother and father. I learned from them the old school way of getting up and working until the job is done. End of story! Thank you for instilling your unbelievable work ethic and drive in me.

To my best friend and business partner Pete Neubig, thanks for living through these life changing experiences with me and having an amazing amount of patience to let me dream the biggest dreams. Also, for letting me think I was always right when we both know I wasn't.

Our business coach Doug Winnie. From day one, he never let up on and always held us accountable. We would not have a business if it wasn't for you, Doug.

Our mentor and business partner, Brad Sugars. You opened our eyes to a world of abundance and exponential growth. Your training and mentoring has made us realize the sky IS the limit.

Chapter 1

Job of My Dreams (But Was It The Job of a Lifetime?)

The day that will live forever in my memory is September 13, 2001. For most people, it would be two days earlier, on what has come to be called 9/11. To date, it is the most horrific attack on US soil. Two days after that historic event is the day that would become my day of reckoning and will be burned into my memory forever. It has become my "Why" in life.

I remember that day well because it was the day my employer, Continental Airlines, notified me that I'd be dispatched to ferry empty airplanes and reposition them to different airports around the country. These planes were grounded after 9/11 and needed to be repositioned so the airline could start transporting the thousands of stranded passengers to their destinations and get back into the business of flying the public again. And, by the way, "you are hereby served a furlough notice along with 1,200 of your closest pilot friends; thanks for playing." Thanks to some crazies hijacking a couple of iron birds and flying them into buildings, the nature of my dream job changed forever.

At the time, only eleven percent of would-be airline pilots taking their first flight lessons went on to become airline pilots for large commercial airlines. I was proud to be a part of that eleven percent.

The date was May 13, 1998. I remember it like it was yesterday. I was twenty-five years old at the time. To say I was in awe of landing my dream job would be an understatement. I was the second youngest pilot hired by Continental Airlines at the time when the average pilot age was thirty-five. Persistence, and the drive to achieve, was ingrained into my DNA from birth, but being an airline prodigy is just one example of how this type-A personality trait has played out in my life.

As early as eight years old, I perused newspapers for stock picks. I'd harass my older sister Donna until she gave in to my repeated requests to call a stockbroker so I could place an order. That's how determined and driven I was, before hitting puberty.

Of course, as you can imagine, the stockbroker on the other end of the phone didn't believe I was old enough to purchase stocks. I wasn't. But that didn't stop me. My mom got on the phone with him and explained that I was serious about buying stock and had her permission to do so. I ended up a proud stakeholder in blue-chip AT&T.

That driven attitude, along with my smartass grin, has been with me until this day. At eleven years old, I learned to lie about my age. From then until thirteen, I lied about my age to get into the gym and work out with my older brother Wayne. I used my brother Marc's school ID card and pretended I was him.

Wayne taught me all about passion and drive. I learned from him during our work out sessions. In one summer, I went from one hundred seventy pounds round to a trim one-forty. I rode my ten- speed bicycle five miles each way to participate in a a nine a.m. aerobics class, swim, play basketball, run the track, and work out with weights. I'd leave my second aerobics class at six p.m. And this was every day.

This drive and determination led me to the world of football in high school. I went to a pretty rough school that placed winning and self-pride highest priorities. That's where I learned what it's like to get my ass kicked hard. More importantly, I learned to get back up and "get on the line" for some more, which turns out to be real valuable in the business world. That "no-shit never-give-up-or-quit attitude is what carried me into my flying lessons. You see, I knew nothing else except attacking something with fury and determination. The average flying lesson course takes four to six years. I accomplished mine in two.

Getting hired, at twenty-two, by a regional airline subsidiary of the once-famous TWA Airlines was a tell-tale sign that my drive wasn't going anywhere—except, perhaps, to the moon! To get there, I had to work hard at getting in my flight hours while working toward my college degree. I got my first flight job before finishing college, which landed me in a unique position at a very critical time in my life.

I didn't know how to go about it, actually. I had a college professor at California State University in Los Angeles who was an airport manager for Hollywood Burbank

Airport. He was the only person I knew in the airline world and I would often go to him for real life advice. He sat me down one day and said, "Steve, in this business, you get a job and a seniority number as quickly as you can. The company you start with will probably not be the one you end up with. Enjoy being an airline pilot and welcome to 'college via correspondence." I received my degree from an accredited college in New Jersey without ever stepping foot on campus. I assume it was legitimate since it ended up on my transcripts and was later accepted by the airlines as a degree in aviation administration.

Having a degree was not a requirement, but, statistically, pilots with a college degree have better odds of landing a job interview with a major airline than those without one. And I wanted to be a pilot for a major airline.

To obtain a captain's certification as an airline pilot, you have to take a test and get what is called an Airline Transport Pilot License. In order to get that license, you had to be at least twenty-three years old. At that age, I already had a long list of flying certifications and accreditations. But I wanted that license, and needed it for the next phase of my career. Age is a minimal factor, however, because you can't become an airline captain without that license. Twenty-three year olds aren't typically in the position to earn that achievement, but I wasn't your typical twenty-three year old. I wanted it as soon as I could get it, and I had the drive to pursue it.

There was a captain's position open at the John F. Kennedy International Airport, one of the busiest airports in the world. The congestion of the New York air space makes L.A. Freeway look like a rural country road.

It wasn't simply the volume of air traffic that flowed in and out of the three busiest airports along the east coast corridor that made that position coveted and challenging. JFK, LaGuardia, and Newark are all within a stone's throw of each other. When you throw in the weather factor, and a kid from Los Angeles with hardly any winter flying experience, that adds up to a very sharp learning curve.

In the airline business, a pilot's career path follows this trajectory: Become a captain at a small regional airline, build up flight hours, then, after a few years, start applying to major airlines. This made no sense to me. I started applying for major airline positions as soon as I earned my college degree, which is essentially checking a box. I checked that box, so it was time to move up. That was my thinking.

At that time, my fiancée, who is now my wife, was living in Huntington Beach, California and I was flying out of New York. That meant I had to catch a flight from our apartment in California to reposition myself in New York so that I could show up for my job assignment. This is called "commuting" and is parallel to someone driving a long distance to get to their job. Flight attendants do the same thing. I consider this one of the benefits to working in the airline industry since it opens up many other job possibilities for airline pilots and flight attendants who want to live in one part of the country and work in another.

This long drawn-out weekly commute from coast to coast is part of the reason I was able to finish my college degree so quickly. I was trapped in a metal tube hurling through the air for six hours at a time, which is a lot like locking someone in a room and making them do their homework. Once I finished college and had my degree in hand, I took the opportunity to fold, stuff, stamp, and seal my resume, sending it to every airline in the world. This was my monthly routine. Either they would tell me "fuck off" or they'd get tired of seeing my resume and invite me to an interview. Either outcome was okay with me. I followed the same routine month after month. The flight attendants who worked this route on a regular basis understood that, when stamps and envelopes made their appearance, I was in my zone and not to be jacked with.

After that process, I received an invitation to interview at Continental Airlines and a subsequent job offer, which I immediately accepted. I promptly learned all I could about the airline. After going through eight weeks of new-hire training, I obtained a position as a flight engineer on a Boeing 727 based out of the Pacific Micronesian island of Guam. We affectionately referred to it as "The Rock."

On the week I finished flight school training, American Airlines, TWA, and Alaska Airlines all called me with job offers. American was, by far, the biggest airline in the industry at the time and, again, I was not sure what to do. I called the only person who ever gave me solid advice, my old college professor. He said, "You made it to the majors. Doing it at twenty-five years old is like a high school kid playing in the NBA." Then he gave me the same words of wisdom he had earlier, as I was about to leave college. "This is a crazy industry, and who you start with most likely will not be the company you end up with. You have your seniority number. If you're happy with the company, ride the wave, but you won't know you made the right choice until the day you retire." I decided to stay with Continental. Welcome to "The Rock."

For three years, I flew out of Guam traveling to the most beautiful and isolated islands on the planet along with routes all over Asia and Australia. This would prove to be useful to me in the future. In July 2001, my wife and I felt that, even though we loved the island-style laid-back living, it was time to head back stateside, so we made the decision to move back to the mainland and plant roots where Continental had its world headquarters, or "Mecca" as we called it.

Houston, Texas is where my story really begins.

Punched in the Mouth

9/11 was as surreal to me as it was to anyone else. I can remember where I was and what I was doing when I heard on the radio that the twin towers had been hit by airplanes. Thinking about it still gives me goosebumps to this day. My view of the world, and life, was very different on September 12, 2011 than it was two days earlier. I went from having the safest, most secure job I could hope for to being punched in the mouth. I realized that safe, secure job was anything but safe or secure.

Something many people don't remember is that, during the hours after the towers fell, every single plane flying anywhere in the world was ordered to land immediately. It did not matter where they were landing, it was going to happen either on the pilot's own volition or by courtesy of the local military. If they failed to do so, there would be fighter jets on their asses forcing them to land. Luckily, I was not flying that day, but many of my pilot friends were. Something else happened in the following days that would make me realize the severity of the circumstances.

On the days following the terrorist attack, all the airlines, including Continental Airlines where I worked as a pilot, dispatched airplanes carrying extra flight crews all around the world to retrieve airplanes and reposition them to various airports. I'll never forget walking through the huge, cavernous airport terminal at Denver International Airport, which was completely empty and eerily quiet due to no passengers boarding planes and no airport personnel working as usual, looking at the hundreds of planes sitting lifeless on the tarmac stacked like a jigsaw puzzle. The constant, steady buzz of commotion was now a cone of silence. There was absolutely no movement in the airport at all, and I remember thinking, "This happy-go-lucky airline pilot without a care in the world is fucked, and life as I know it is over."

Though I had not been given an official furlough notice, I had come to realize that I was not qualified to do anything else. It's scary, when you have focused your entire life on learning a specific skill, to imagine yourself in a position where that skill can no longer be used. When everything you've trained for seems useless, you feel like your back is in a corner. And that's a dark, scary place to be.

Being an airline pilot was my life. It was an amazing and rewarding career, and would continue to be as long as there were airlines. But when 9/11 happened, I realized how vulnerable I was. When that weakness shows itself, it shines like a beacon in your face, blinding you to everything else. Facing the possibility of a furlough, with the very real possibility of getting kicked out on the street without a job, along with thousands of other airline pilots more qualified than me, was a scary feeling. It felt even worse when I realized I wasn't qualified for any other occupation.

I learned something interesting about the human mind from all of this. Adversity pushes people to the limits. The fight-or-flight impulse kicks in. Most people would cling desperately to what they know, like hanging on to a sinking ship instead of braving the choppy waters and swimming to safety. Instead of surviving, they'd go down with the ship. Not me. But, I remember thinking, "I can fly a one hundred million dollar airplane around the world, and take on the responsibility for thousands of lives, but I'm not qualified to drive a commercial truck." I later learned this is called a "Zero-Option Mentality."

Admittedly, at first I felt like a victim. I wanted to go down with the ship instead of swimming the turbulent waters. Some of my pilot friends went back to small, regional airlines to make a quarter of the salary they were making at Continental. Others went to Korea or China so they could remain employed. And then the layoffs came.

When that happened, I ended up being thirty seniority numbers from the bottom of the 5,500-person list. I revisited the words of wisdom I got from my college professor: "Get a seniority number as soon as you can."

A buddy of mine got hired by Continental two weeks ahead of me. He delayed his start date because he wanted to take a vacation with his family prior to leaving that current job. When that happened, I got his slot and he got a slot in the next month's training class. When the company furloughed people off the seniority list, the class behind me got the axe first. My friend was furloughed for over two years, but I escaped because he took a vacation. That proved to be a valuable lesson to me.

At that moment, the allure--or should I say, the illusion--of having a safe and secure job was anything but that. In fact, having such specialized training made me more vulnerable than someone with multiple talents. Perhaps that is what employers want, good employees that do what they are told and cling to the security of a paycheck rather than engage in out-of-the-box thinking like an entrepreneur in control of his own destiny.

Post 9/11: A New World Requires a New Way of Thinking

It was clear to me then that, even if things worked out in my airline career, I was one terrorist attack, disaster, or board of director meeting away from losing my job. It was amazing how quickly, for the sake of shareholders, judges would abrogate union contracts and employees would be forced to take wage cuts while having their pensions wiped away. At Continental, instead of going into bankruptcy, the employees agreed to freeze our pensions and end company contributions in order to keep our jobs.

The sad part was, the terrorist attack had nothing to do with our job performance or the professionalism we brought to the table. I started looking at other options.

One option I considered was real estate. It seemed like a natural gravitation. I liked the idea of owning rental property. Logically, it made sense to get paid over and over again for the same amount of work. Secondly, I liked the thought of a tenant paying down my mortgage while property values went up. I also quickly learned that many people of substantial wealth earned the bulk of that wealth owning real estate in one shape or form. It was a simple business model and a great financial leverage tool in good times or bad. After all, everyone needs a roof over their head. In good times and bad, this is a basic human need.

Since I had a lot of time off between flight schedules, it seemed to fit that way too. Since I knew my career was in jeopardy, I needed to figure out another way of making income. It became my life's mission real quickly to solve this problem for myself and my family.

I had met pilots over the years who had owned rental properties, but I didn't know any of them well enough to ask for their help. I'm the type of person that, when I put my mind to something, I get so focused that I will talk to anyone and everyone about the subject. When you are locked in a metal tube 30,000 feet above ground for three to six hours at a time, you find something to do to occupy your time. I was either reading about real estate or talking to the other pilot to see if they had any information that I could soak up. Of course, I got a mixed bag of responses. Some would say they wished they had started earlier. Others said they didn't have the drive. And a few more said they tried it and failed, so they'd never do it again. I honed in on the pilots who said they owned rental properties and enjoyed it. I asked them questions till they told me to shut up.

I was also curious about the pilots who had tried real estate investing and failed. To me, failure was not an option, but I like to know the full story. I had an opportunity to listen to experience and hear other people's drama, so I took it.

The common theme from the failed investors is what they did wrong. It wasn't just one thing. They all took several missteps that caused an implosion which resulted in their failure. I noticed a common theme among the ones who were successful and another common theme among the ones who failed.

There was a whole culture of real estate investing among pilots that was invisible to me until I started asking questions. I wanted to learn as much as I could, so I started going to the library. It felt funny getting a library card, but I honestly didn't know where else to go. I'd go to pick up books on real estate and self development in my pilot uniform, and the looks I got from people was comical. Some of the people appeared confused. One elderly gentleman asked if I was the new car valet service he had requested through the library's comment card box. I told him I was not, but I would be happy to park his car for him anyways.

In 2001, the online real estate market was not quite as developed as it is now, and I wasn't clear how to get into it. I had to learn a whole new language. I started with a yearning to learn (my why), and attacked it with the same mental toughness I used when playing high school and junior college football, and when I obtained my pilot's license. I set a goal, just like I did when searching for an airline captain position with a major airline, and hit it with my characteristic no-quit zero-option mental attitude and full-throttle-through-the-wall mindset.

After junior college, I had taken an interest in bodybuilding. Through football and bodybuilding, I learned the art of self-discipline. I learned how to stick with something even if I wasn't naturally gifted at it. I also learned how to approach things I was not comfortable doing. I started working out at the age of thirteen and dedicated myself to learning everything I could about it. That's how I approached real estate.

I began to read one book per week. My days and nights were consumed with learning all I could. I felt like I was so far behind and needed to catch up, it was my duty to myself and my family to learn this real estate game as soon as I could. I had to take action as quickly as possible, especially since I was hanging by a thread on the seniority list at the airline. One hiccup and I would be out of a job. I did not know exactly what it would look like, but I knew that real estate was my future.

I love how Robert Kiyosaki said, "Mind your business," which means work your day job and spend nights and weekends keeping your mind on your own business. That's exactly what I did. I flew planes and, on the side, learned as much as I could by focusing my mind on my own real estate business.

Foray Into Flipping

All the reading and learning I got into boiled down to one word: "Action." That was the missing ingredient, and seemingly the common thread, among all the fellow pilots I had talked to who did not succeed. Now, of course, we all know that there are varying degrees of action. There's Right Action, there's Wrong Action, and there's No Action, which is the most common.

So many people choose the path of no action because they fear making a mistake or looking bad. They'd rather stay in their current awful predicament than to venture out and try something new. To a certain degree, I've been in each of those groups at various times in my life. I will admit, the Chicken Little in me was scared to risk all the money I had on a down payment for a rental property when I was still teetering on the precipice of unemployment.

I was still clinging to the old way of thinking, hoping my employer would swoop in and take care of their employees so I could go back to my happy-go-lucky life. Of course, the tragedy of 9/11 was real, and the airlines' dire situation was getting worse. After they canceled our pensions and retirement plans, they came back for a second round of "Screw the Pilot" by offering us a concessionary contract. They wanted to cut our pay so they could outsource our jobs to the regional airlines because that was the lower-cost solution. I remember the CEO of Continental Airlines threatening to park airplanes and furlough more employees if we didn't take the pay cut. Their goal was to make the shareholders happy. So we could take the bad deal or the worse deal. At least we had a choice.

Two things became clear: First, that safe and secure job I thought I had was not safe or secure. Secondly, airline executives would do whatever it to took to protect their own positions before they thought about rank and file. A storm was on the horizon and it was getting darker by the day, and headed right towards my livelihood.

That reality reiterated, in my mind, why it was so important to control my own destiny. I had to figure out a way to control my destiny and not be dependent on someone else for my livelihood, let alone my family's financial security. My employer's objectives clearly did not align with my own.

While studying more about taking action and still scared to make the commitment, I learned about an interesting real estate strategy that allows an investor to be in real estate but not one hundred percent with their own money. It's called an options contract. Without getting technical, the idea is to find a motivated seller and buy an option to purchase the property with a forty-five day window. This meant I had the option to buy the property, but not the obligation to buy the property. The seller, on the other hand, was obligated to sell it to me or anyone of my choosing as long as I assigned my right to buy the property to that individual. And the best part is this: I could invest in real estate without getting my own money involved. That was the plan. Later, I learned that strategy is not technically investing but is more like a job.

This was when home sellers were having a difficult time finding buyers in Houston, around 2003, but with the right database of buyers, it was much easier. I would buy an option then promote the home to my database of investors looking to buy. My profit margin was the difference between the buy price stated in the options contract and the sell price I agreed to with my buyer. Once I found the buyer, I would "assign" my options rights over to the buyer for a fee that I would receive after the property closed. I never actually took ownership of the property.

As with anything else in life, I was totally committed and focused on doing the best job I could by taking massive action. I learned as much as I could about options buying and selling, taking courses on how to do it successfully and booking time with my mentors. I looked for any way I could systemize the process and leverage the business model. I even took several negotiation courses and learned communication techniques such as Neuro Linguistic Programming (NLP), along with other communication tools in order to sharpen my negotiation skills.

Growing up, I was good at convincing people to get excited about a vision I had, but now I was getting a chance to practice those skills and enhance them even more. I played that game for roughly three years. While I did make quite a bit of money, I realized that it was also a job. As soon as I stopped working, the money stopped pouring in. That was not the goal. I already had a job as an airline pilot, and real estate was becoming an extension of that job. It became a time suck for my family and me. I wanted more passive income, and with a newly developed skill, I was ready to up my game.

Getting Into Apartments

In 2004, as a part of my continuous education goals, I joined a local real estate investment club and started to learn about passive income investing. This club was geared mostly towards apartment complex investments than single-family rentals. Although they did help with single-family properties, it was not their main focus. Again, this required learning a whole new language. While there are similarities between single-family and multi-family properties, the business models are very different.

The more I learned about apartments, the more I wanted to get out of flipping properties and use the money I earned to buy an apartment complex. I started to look around at what I could afford, and what was on the market, but the investment opportunities that existed weren't in my price range. At the time, the price point per door in Houston only made good investment sense, including purchasing and staffing the apartment complex, if the complex had seventy-five doors or more (the term "door" means "unit" in the real estate world). The cost of that type of investment was not something I could afford at the time. The smaller properties, composed of ten to thirty doors, were time-intensive investments. There just isn't enough cash flow to staff them properly. So what happens is the investor finds a tenant who is an alpha male (or female) and they become the eyes and ears of the investor. They let you know the good tenants, bad tenants, problem children, and the things that need fixing around the complex. So, basically, they are the mother hen of the coop.

Typically, the mother hen is there to be the base of operations. They offer to collect rent and do some light maintenance, if they have the skills. In some situations, the husband is the resident handyman in the evening, because he has his regular job, and the wife collects the rent and handles issues of a personal nature. It sounds like a match made in heaven, however (and you knew this was coming), it's not all chocolate and roses.

Here's something to think about: You've just spent your life savings, or close to it, on this small apartment complex. You're now responsible for hundreds of thousands of dollars in debt and mortgage payments, and you have a business worth at least several hundred thousand dollars, maybe even multiple millions. The person running your business, essentially the CEO, is there because they were the loudest, most outgoing, and perhaps the most vocal tenant when you purchased the property. Maybe they opposed potential rent changes, or they were vocal in requesting maintenance and upgrades. Either way, they were the mouthpiece for the rest of the community. There was no job interview, no qualifications required, no screening, and no certification or demonstrated knowledge of legal property code, eviction laws, fair housing, or anything else. Unfortunately, this is how most new investors in the apartment world start out, and this business model shockingly fails.

Not only that, but the new owner now has the added responsibility of fixing whatever problems the last manager/tenant caused. That means the property owner basically has a job, and a pretty crappy one at that. This is definitely not a passive investment, which is what most people who go into real estate (myself included) are searching for.

As I was learning more about owning apartment complexes, an available property came up for sale. It was a sixteen unit apartment complex in Houston's Third Ward. The Third Ward is a part of Houston's inner city that has not yet been re-gentrified. That's a nice way of saying the property was in the ghetto and was going to be tough to manage.

Since I was a part of an investing group where many members owned apartments all around the city, I was able to talk with fellow members about their properties and hear the good, the bad, and the ugly stories that go along with owning real estate. I was told that around the corner from my apartment complex, there was a member who owned a fifty-two door complex and he'd be more than happy to talk with me about the area, and about my deal in particular. So I met with him.

I stood in the parking lot of this guy's fifty-two door apartment complex with my wife next to me holding my six month old son while this guy shot holes in my dreams, explaining why that sixteen door apartment complex was a bad investment. He said, "This is not something you want to get into." His first-hand experience with the neighborhood meant that he was dealing with the same problems I would have on a much larger scale if I purchased that property. Little did I know at the time that this other investor would become my best friend and lifelong business partner. His name was Pete Neubig.

I took Pete's advice and didn't buy the property. He called me a month later and told me he was looking at buying a thirty-nine door complex in a better area. He was looking for partners. He wanted to know if I'd be interested in being a passive investor on the deal. Three months later, at the beginning of 2005, I was a one-quarter partner in an apartment complex.

Come to think of it, maybe Pete was the best salesperson of all. He sold me on not buying that sixteen door complex and going into partnership with him instead.

Since I was a passive investor, all I had to do was put my money up, and contribute more if necessary, in what they call a cash call. I wasn't required to do anything else. But I wanted to learn everything I could about real estate investing. I told Pete I'd be a partner if he would let me be more hands on in running the apartment complex. Not one to turn down free labor, he agreed. Scott, the owner of the complex, owned approximately 1,200 doors in four different apartment complexes, so he was another investor I was hoping to learn from. All he wanted to do was free up some capital for other investments, so, instead of selling the thirty-nine doors outright, he divested himself of his ownership stake in exchange for some cash to buy another apartment complex. He effectively became the passive investor in our deal.

When I agreed to that deal, I didn't realize the apartment complex was landlocked between a private school and a church. Both entities had at some point expressed an interest in acquiring the property to expand their own. The entire neighborhood was being revitalized. People were tearing down older homes and building very nice, expensive Victorian-style houses for three times the price of the current homes, most of which were neglected or barely standing.

Scott firmly believed that either the school or the church would eventually make a solid offer on the apartment complex. That's why he didn't fully want to exit the deal. He was right. Six months later, the church made a decent offer. The interesting thing is, the apartment complex was purchased with a conduit loan, which is a Wall Street-backed loan that cannot be paid off early. That meant the church had to wait two years before taking ownership. That suited us fine, and it fit into their timeline. They put up $40,000 as non-refundable earnest money, and we held and operated the property for two years.

The best thing about doing business with a church is they pay with cash. That was our saving grace because, if you do the math, our closing date fell right in the middle of the Great Recession of 2007.

They never batted an eye. The church's plan was to level the building and make it a parking lot. Our contractual obligation to them was to let the leases expire and hand the property over empty. I guess a church kicking thirty-nine families out of their homes to construct a parking doesn't make good press.

The sale went off as planned. We were then fat, dumb, and happy, and sitting on extra cash while the rest of the free world was falling off the financial cliff. Pete and I had a good relationship, and we both felt that our goals were aligned, so we decided to continue our business relationship into our next venture. In 2007, Houston property owners were having a fire sale. It seemed like a good time to acquire single-family properties. What could go wrong? We had just sold an apartment complex, so we were savvy investors. Right?

This is where our story begins.

Chapter 2

Going Ghetto Fabulous

Pete and I started looking look for our next investment opportunity. One day, he approached me and said, "Hey, I found these great deals that nobody seems to be interested in." That should have been his first clue, or "red flag," as we say in the flying world. "They have low purchase prices and, on paper, they appear to have a high cash-on-cash return. These look like the price point is low enough that there will always be a rental market for them. They're called "low-income-high-cash-flow rental properties."

Well, he got it half right. They definitely were low income. In more ways than one.

For one thing, on paper, these investments were fantastic. Logically, they made sense. The initial acquisition was quite low, roughly $40,000, and the value of the homes were about $60,000 to $65,000 with some closer to $80,000. So, from that perspective, the equity capture was very good. The properties rented in the range of $800 to $900 per month. On paper, they appeared to show plenty of upside. At least, the numbers were right.

Now, I knew that if we were going down this road, we could not simply buy one property. This had to be done in volume. That made sense to me. Remember, I'm a massive action kind of guy.

We ended up purchasing twenty properties within the first year. Shortly after that, we got a better understanding of why other investors weren't interested in these properties, and why the investors who had them before us were ready to unload them. These low-end properties opened up a Pandora's box of huge problems we never knew existed, and did not know how to shut.

The first reason people do not own these types of investment properties is because of the clientele. Please understand, it's not that they were bad people, or even bad tenants for that matter, but they were living paycheck to paycheck. That is just a fact of life for some people, neither good nor bad. It just is.

As landlords, we believed rent should be a top priority. But people living paycheck to paycheck don't always see it that way. They have their own ideas about managing money, and it took us a while to see things from their perspective.

For instance, putting gas in the car is, and should be, a top priority. If you go to put gas in your car but don't have any money, guess what, you don't get any gas. That's not a striking concept to most people.

One thing I noticed is these people love their cars. Some of them had nicer cars than I did as an airline pilot. It was almost comical when I would drive up to collect their rent. They would joke with me about my car, saying things like, "Maybe I should pay more rent so you can get a better hooptie for riding around in the hood." I'd laugh, but inside, I was scratching my head.

Another concern these people have is keeping their utilities on. If you're living paycheck to paycheck, making a low income (maybe even minimum wage), and you are faced with whether or not to pay rent or keep the electricity flowing, you'll likely keep the electric on because it's cheaper, which means you can keep more money in your pocket. And if you're facing the possibility of eviction, you may not even do that because why pay for something you aren't going to use?

Then there's food to eat, clothes to wear, emergencies, etc. In other words, the basic necessities of life.

Low-income people have a lot of financial decisions to make with just a little bit of money, so they have to set their priorities based on their income and the harsh realities of their living environment. It's a different kind of thinking than an airline pilot is used to. Someone told me once that I have "first-world" problems, not the same kinds of problems as my tenants. I don't agree because I'm giving them shelter, which is a basic human need, and I am financially responsible for it all.

I don't think low-income people intentionally plan to skip paying rent. What happens is, they have $1,500 in bills and a $1,000 paycheck. They have to prioritize their commitments knowing they must also buy groceries. They have to think, who has to get paid now, and who I can let slide?

I got schooled on this economic reality very early on. If the landlord or property owner doesn't set the expectation that they are a priority on getting paid when the rent is due, then they likely aren't getting paid. That rental property will either remain vacant or it will have a tenant with constant struggles in paying rent. Eventually, that tenant will get evicted, but not until the landlord has suffered months of frustration, wasted time, endless lies, and massive headaches with sleepless nights.

Pete used to say, "Look at their past and you will see their future." I try to see the good in people. I thought he was just being negative, but time and time again he proved to be right. People don't change unless they want to or there is a compelling motivation.

Very early on, when we had roughly a dozen properties, I would get excited around the first of the month. I would get in my car, drive around, and pick up the rent from all the tenants (well, from the ones who decided to pay it that month, at least).

One day, Pete said to me, "What are you doing? You're letting them train you on how they operate. They have been renters their whole life. You have been a landlord for a fraction of that time. They know when rent is due. Either you are training them how the business operates or they are training you on how they operate."

I took that into consideration, but I still liked to get the money in my hand because I felt, on some level, that I could make a difference and, since I am an action-oriented person, I drove my route. Frustration set in when I would go to a house and see cars in the driveway only to have nobody answer the door. When I'd call them, the number would be disconnected. Then they would call me from some new phone number and tell me they'd have rent on Friday. You can guess what happened when I drove to their house on Friday. Sure enough, they wouldn't have the rent, and their phone number was disconnected. Round and round we went.

During this time, we had an average tenancy of eight months, and maintenance costs were three times the rent amount. Whenever a tenant would leave, which they did very often, not only would they take their personal belongings with them, but they would take parting gifts with them. That drove up our maintenance costs because we had to replace those items, and we often had to rebuild a large part of the house's interior in the process.

Some of the things they took included copper wiring, air conditioning units, refrigerators, ceiling fans, light bulbs, whatever they could get their hands on. If the tenants didn't take things, then the neighbors would come and help themselves to items after the tenants moved out. It was like a free swap meet.

Almost every time a tenant moved out, we would have to replace carpets, wiring, and air conditioning units.

We tried so hard to keep those air conditioning units. It became a battle of wills. It was like a chess match to see who could outsmart whom. It's important to note that these were not three-ton HVAC systems. These were small window cooling units, but as much as we secured them, embedded them into walls, or welded cages around them, people always seemed to find a way to get these $99 air conditioning units. What is it that people say when going over something that doesn't really matter? "It's not the money, it's the principle." Well, I call bullshit on that one. It's the money!

We could never figure out how to fix that problem. We must have bought enough air conditioning units during that time to cool southeast Houston. I'd think to myself, if only they would spend that much time and energy toward something good, how successful they might be. The reality was, they were probably more successful than we were. At least at the air conditioning game.

There were times when I wondered if the appliance store guy had a scam running. Maybe he'd steal the A/C units and sell them back to us. He always seemed so happy when we walked in, and knew exactly what we were looking for.

As you can imagine, by this time, we were in a bad way. It was a vicious cycle, and we couldn't get ourselves out of it. Tenants vacated properties too often, and the more it happened the more desperate we'd become. At one point, our vacancy rate shot up to thirty percent and hovered there for a what felt like and eternity. In case you're wondering, that's unsustainable. But we were working so hard in the wrong direction that we never stopped to realize it and just kept on pushing.

We became desperate for good tenants, we'd do anything to get them. Everything we learned about real estate investing until then went out the window. If someone showed up with money in hand, we rented to them. We offered two weeks free rent and no-deposit specials. We advertised "Bad Credit OK" just to make the phone ring, and it did. Unfortunately, all it got us was more bad tenants.

These tenants would stay in the property for a month or so, then when rent came due, they wouldn't pay. And we'd have to go through the legal process to evict them. Throughout that process, the tenants were still living in our house for free, and we never saw a penny of the rent money owed to us.

In Houston, to evict someone is a complicated and drawn out process. You can't just kick them out. Rent may be due on the first of the month, but it isn't technically late until the third. A landlord cannot start an eviction process until day four when he sends a three-day eviction letter. The landlord can't file for eviction at the county courthouse until at least the seventh of the month. Meanwhile, the tenant is living rent-free.

Landlords can't get an eviction court date until the twenty-first day of the month. If rent hasn't been paid, he'll win his case, but a writ of possession isn't filed until the twenty-eighth of the month. On the thirtieth, the tenant is given twenty-four to forty-eight hours to vacate the property. The constable will forcibly remove the tenant if they're not out by the fifth of the following month, but how soon he does this depends on his own workload and the calendar. Long weekends and holidays can delay the process. It could be the fifteenth of the next month before the tenant is actually out of the property. Now the landlord has lost two months rent, and he has to clean up the property and get it ready for the next tenants. By the time he rents it again he could have lost three months rent.

The root cause of our headaches and constant frustration, we later realized, was crystal clear. We were picking the wrong tenants. This is the key to a successful landlording business model. The primary challenge is, there just aren't many good tenants in this rent range. Yes, the pond is full of fish, but it's the quality of the catch that is important, not the quantity.

You would think two intelligent (or should I say "semi-intelligent?") men would have realized the problem and found a solution. You might also think that, based on our experiences, we would realize this type or rental property wasn't the sweet snack we thought it would be and look for an exit strategy. We finally decided to take action. We did two things that made matters worse for us.

First, we decided to double down and buy more of the same type of properties. In fact, we bought another fifteen low-income properties. Our thinking went like this: Since we are halfway through the mountain, let's just push through to the other side. We thought having more volume would leverage economies of scale and make our situation better. In reality, we were pouring gasoline on a raging fire, and it exploded right in our faces. Things went from bad to worse in a matter of months. It got so bad that my wife told me, "If you buy another property, it better be a nice one because you will be living in it."

Well, Houston had a problem tenant and his name was "Ike."

Hurricane Ike: Bastard, Savior, and Friend

Having a tropical storm develop in the Gulf of Mexico was not an uncommon occurrence, but in September 2008, it turned out to be a different kind of a storm. I turned on the news to see that a tropical disturbance was developing. Its name "Ike."

Ike was gaining strength and the storm gurus predicted it would head straight toward Houston. It was getting more national attention on the news than most tropical storms because it followed on the heels of Hurricane Katrina, which was a major catastrophe for the city of New Orleans. The storm grew into a Category 5 storm and was, in fact, heading directly toward Houston.

This was my first experience with a Hurricane. I was amazed at what I saw unfolding before my eyes. The city went into a frenzy as local authorities evacuated the town. People raided stores, taking everything from water to gasoline, and clearing the shelves of all sorts of merchandise. It was both interesting and scary at the same time. I was so mesmerized by the events that I didn't concern myself with our rental properties. My first priority was the safety and security of my family.

The storm hit on Saturday evening. I had arrived home from a flight to Hawaii that morning. Soon after landing, they shut the airport down. That night, the storm hit with a fury. It drove right up the center of the city and ripped everything in its path. It was common in Houston to have "hurricane parties," so my family stayed at a friend's house that night. The next morning, we drove back to our house to survey the damage. I was in awe.

Growing up in Los Angeles, I had experienced some of Mother Nature's tirades and seen first hand what damage an earthquake could cause. But a hurricane is not an earthquake. The winds that pounded the city all night renewed my respect for Mother Nature. I got to see what a Category 5 hurricane can do. That bitch uprooted one-hundred-year-old trees like weeds from a vegetable garden. It still amazes me to this day when I think about it.

Now that the storm had passed, it was time to see what emergencies I had to deal with from the rental properties. Pete and I met up to drive the properties and perform a damage assessment. Over twenty homes had major roof damage, several took on water damage from flooding, and we couldn't get to some of them because the water level was too high. I felt bad for the tenants, the families, who lived in those rental properties because they wouldn't have a home anymore.

Then it hit me like a punch to the gut. If they can't live in these homes anymore, how could we expect them to pay rent? How will we pay our mortgages? Pete and I must have been thinking this at the same time. As that thought entered my mind, he said, "We're screwed. We're going to have to sell off these properties to avoid going bankrupt." Talk about a quiet, uneasy drive.

The situation wasn't pretty, and the more properties we visited, the worse it got. There was no way even I, the happy-go-lucky airline pilot who sees the good in everything, could put a positive spin on this dire situation. My instincts kicked in. Everything I learned as an airline pilot, how to deal with emergencies in the cockpit and flying in difficult situations, kicked in (it would show up later to help us again when Hurricane Harvey came to visit).

I said to Pete, "We need to find a solution to this problem fast. Let's break it down and give it a full assessment. We'll start at the beginning and look for solutions that won't kill us."

That's exactly what we did. By the way, that's how we handle emergencies in the aviation world.

We checked each property to see which ones could be fixed the quickest to keep the rent money coming in so we could pay our bills. The ones that had major damage would have to wait. We systematically made our way through a check list of properties. Being new to the rental business, we missed one vital step in our haste to take action. More experienced investors reminded us of this step, and that was our saving grace.

"Have you guys called your insurance company to file your claim?" one investor asked.

We had such tunnel vision, hell bent on fixing the problem, that we completely forgot we had insurance. That kind of damage was precisely the reason we paid our monthly premiums. So we called our insurance agent and the first thing she said was, "I've been waiting for your call. You are the last investors to call about damage to rental homes." You would think that a part of being an insurance agent after a major catastrophe would be to reach out to clients and see what help they need.

In the end, we got twenty new roofs and much of the storm damage was covered. The lessons we learned proved to be invaluable in August 2017 when Hurricane Harvey came knocking. On a side note, we did get to experience one of the homes catching fire and burning down, so there's that.

I remember it like it was yesterday. All day, every day after the hurricane, we dealt with one emergency after another. It was like a game of Whack-A-Mole. As soon as we would deal with one emergency, another one would pop up. One morning, I woke up to sixteen missed calls from the same phone number. "There is no way this could be good," I said to myself.

As I listened to the voicemails in the order they came in, it was like a play by play of the disaster unfolding in real time, and every message was worse than the last. The first message was the tenant calling to let me know they didn't have power inside the house. With the hurricane running its rampant path through Houston, that was no shock. My family was without power for two weeks.

The second message was a frantic voice yelling that they had lit a candle and the drapes caught on fire. Third call was, "The house is on fire!"

At this point, I remember saying out loud (to my voicemail), "Call the fucking fire department!"

The last and final call was the tenant telling me the house burnt down and was gone. I was in shock, and I'm sure if you were watching, you'd have seen my jaw dropped wide open while I listened to this drama play out on my voicemail. When I called the tenant back, I could hear the fire trucks in the background, and all the tenant could say was, "Man, I'm sorry. I was just trying to get some light in the house." Then he hung up.

There was nothing left to talk about, I guess. All of his family's cherished belongings were gone, along with my investment property, because of a crooked candle that fell over.

The next thought I had was, how am I going to tell Pete? I thought it would put him over the edge, send him into Crazy Land after the week we just went through. I looked at the phone for several minutes trying think of a positive way to spin this to ease the blow of this devastating news. Finally, I realized that wasn't going to happen, so I said "fuck it" and picked up the phone.

Pete answered right away. My plan of leaving a voicemail went up in smoke. I said, "Pete, we have a big problem." He did not even respond. All I heard was dead silence on the other end of the line. I thought he dropped dead right there before I could even tell him. "Are you there?" I asked.

"Yes."

This was getting worse by the moment. I said, "One of the houses burned down."

Pete's response was the polar opposite of what I expected. "Was anyone hurt?" he asked.

"No."

"Well, that's great news then!"

I thought he was being sarcastic, but I could tell how his voice lifted that he was happy. I asked him, "Did you hear what I said? One of the houses burned down. It's gone."

He asked which one. I told him the address and he was even happier than before. "That's great," he said. "I hated that house."

I thought, either he doesn't understand what "burned down" means or he has lost it. Either way, there was nothing good coming from this conversation.

Then he explained to me that the house was insured for much more than we bought it for. We bought it from another investor for fifty percent of its value, but it was insured for the full value. Pete went on to explain that a fire in this scenario could save us financially. It turned out he was right. Again.

After several months of insurance inspectors and adjusters filtering in and out, we got the mortgage paid off. We were able to get most of the homes we owned repaired from insurance claims and almost all the roofs replaced. We then sold the plot to another investor we knew. He tore down the house and rebuilt a brand new home, a nice one for the ghetto, and everyone came out ahead. Hurricane Ike, bastard that he was, saved us.

Signs, Signs, Everywhere Signs

Let's get back to our rental story.

That era was a unique and scary time in my life. In my heart, I felt that the only way I could solve the problems and overcome the challenges I had was by rolling up my sleeves and making it happen. Back to my catchword: Action. You know, bulldoze my way through them like a true Type-A personality. I simply could not accept failure. I was going to will it to work with every ounce of will I had. Unfortunately, I was trying to force a round peg into a square hole with a blindfold on my head. In hindsight, it was my own emotions--fear of failure, to be precise--that drove me to react to circumstances the way I did. I ran on pure fear and perpetual adrenaline rushes. What I really needed to do was slow down and look at things from a logical business perspective. And develop a singular focus.

When I finally did stop to think, the first thing I did was address the main thing that was killing us. My years of flight training taught me how to deal with emergencies calmly and methodically--

"Aviate, Navigate, Communicate."

Aviate, Navigate, Communicate is the unwritten code that pilots live by. That means, if the plane is off course and on fire, then the pilot tries to communicate with an air traffic control tower. You put out the fire, get back on course, and then call ATC.

Keeping tenants for just eight months was a huge problem because, financially, it was crashing our plane. I tackled it head on. I was sure my proactive guerilla marketing tactics were going to fix it. I read as much as I could on how to create a marketing buzz. I learned every way to make the phone ring. When there is only one person calling to rent your vacant home, you'll perform all sorts of mental gymnastics to justify why that person is a good fit even when you know they would never be acceptable if you had more qualified candidates, which we did not.

I learned very quickly that many people prefer to work with a property owner than a real estate agent when renting a home. The reason is because real estate agents are detached and home owners are not. It's easier to negotiate with a homeowner. Plus, many property owners don't use real estate agents because they don't want to pay leasing fees when they can act as their own landlord.

Renters get blinded by the thousands of standard "For Rent" and "For Sale" signs that look too much alike. I read a study on the internet (so it must be true) that the average person drives by more than one hundred & fifty for sale/for rent signs every day and never notices them. So I decided to create a home-made sign that attracted people's attention. It gave them a compelling reason to pick up the phone and call me. I later learned it's called a Call To Action, or CTA for short.

The homestyle "For Rent" signs I made were crafted out of cardboard. To say that they were just signs would be an understatement. In my mind, I knew these signs were going to get the job done. My motto was "go big or go home." I went big.

I created an assembly line in my garage made up of several stations where I performed each part of the process. First, I used fluorescent construction paper, which I bought at the local Hobby Lobby or Walmart, and big fat black permanent markers. Next, I went to Home Depot and asked if I could take the cardboard boxes they were throwing away. I also purchased a buttload of thirty-six inch wooden spikes. The signs ended up being 24 x 24 inches.

I would mark the fluorescent construction paper with my message using the permanent markers, then I'd glue them to the cardboard and staple them as a secondary way of securing them. If I only glued them or stapled them, the wind would rip them apart, or the rain would cause the glue not to stick. After much trial and error, and many hours of testing, I came to realize that it had to be a combination of the two for it to work right. Finally, I nailed the signs onto the wooden stakes with roofing nails and, just like that, I had homemade yard signs.

The message on the signs was very important. I'd write "Rent Special, Bad Credit OK, Deposit Special, Must See." The idea was to spark an interest. I used action terms to get people to call. For instance, "Call today! First month free."

The phone number would be the biggest thing on the sign. I'd write "3 bedroom/2 bath" for the description, which would be the smallest thing on the sign. I'd never include an address, for two reasons. First, I wanted people to call since we always had several vacant homes. That way, I'd be able to use the signs for another home, if necessary. Secondly, I could use the signs in any area of town. When I made signs, I would spend half the day making as many as I could and create a huge stockpile to use whenever and wherever I needed them.

I used fluorescent paper because certain colors catch people's attention more than others. Fluorescent green, yellow, and orange fit into this category, and the fact that I could buy them in bundles at a discount was a huge bonus. I made them look homemade because I did not want to look like a business. There were two reasons for this: First, as I stated earlier, most people drive by "For Rent" and "For Sale" signs all the time and do not even notice them. The second reason is that, technically, home renters are not supposed to put signs up in certain city limits without a permit, but officials are more apt to let a person with just one "For Rent" sign get away with breaking that rule. Perception is everything, and I wanted to look like I was just an average person desperate (not too far from reality) to get people to call. And call they did.

The next step in the "signology" process was to put the signs out. This involved going from neighborhood to neighborhood where my rental houses were located. I'd start at the house and work my way out in concentric circles around the property, going block by block and street by street. The task was to go out with thirty, forty, and sometimes fifty signs and put them anywhere people were forced to stop. The big idea: When a vehicle approached a stop sign or a traffic light and had to stop, there'd be my sign, and they'd see it.

The tricky part was doing this in the worst parts of the Houston ghetto. The best time to perform this covert operation was at three or four in the morning, before the early bird got his worm. The reason for this is very simple: Nobody was awake at that time. The drug dealers and gangsters normally called it a night after the bars let out at 2 a.m. Also, there was little to no traffic, because people were not yet going to work, so I wouldn't be bothered.

Imagine a white middle-aged male, an airline pilot, driving around the ghetto at three o'clock in the morning with signs in the back of his truck, stopping at all the four-corner intersections and pounding signs into the ground at record speed. That made life interesting, to say the least.

Once the signs were placed, I would easily get fifty to sixty calls in a single day. It got to the point where calls came in so fast I couldn't answer all of them. It was a good problem to have, but it was still a problem. I solved this challenge by getting a seperate phone number that went straight to voicemail. Then I'd call people back as soon as I could. I called it "dialing for dollars."

At one point, I was getting so many calls that I hired a real estate agent to take them for me. Some people might say that was a smart thing to do. It's called leverage. The other side of that argument was the real estate agent was doing a poor job of selecting tenants. We had so many vacancies that we needed a full-time agent to handle it. He became our primary agent because we had plenty of rental properties with an average tenant lease of eight months. That agent got all of our properties to lease, and he would do it at a discount for us because we gave him a huge volume of business, which, for the record, was not necessarily a good thing. In order to get these properties leased, we offered a lot of discount specials and worked out payment deals for tenants. We were that desperate (and so were they). Unfortunately, we lost a lot of money doing that.

One lesson we learned the hard way is that desperation leads to a reactive mindset. A reactive mindset leads to unpredictability. That leads to chaos, which leads to losing money and ultimately alot of sleepless nights.

Looking back at the mistakes we made at that time in our lives, I can see how emotionally attached we were to the business. We were living in desperation, and there was no logical way that business model, or lack thereof, was going to work. When teaching others about the real estate business, I stress this lesson to drive the point home. It was a very dark time in my life.

Being too emotionally close to a problem causes a professional, or anyone for that matter, to think illogically. It leads to reacting out of fear, and when we react out of fear, it is difficult to succeed. That was the problem we had. Pete and I were running out of money, and we were running out of options. In flying terms, it's called a "Coffin Corner." That's when an aircraft is at an altitude that it can't handle. The mach buffet (the speed of the airflow over the aircraft's wing) and stall speed (the lowest speed a plane can fly to stay level) are close to the same. When that happens, the plane falls out of the sky, hence the horrific name. We were putting ourselves in our own coffin corner and didn't know what to do to fix it. The higher we tried to climb, the less cash flow we had in or bank accounts. This all came to a head one afternoon.

Our Famous "Breaking Point" Day

To truly understand the impact this event had on my life, you need to understand the situation. We had a property, deep in the ghetto, and the tenant never paid the rent on time. From Day 1, she always had some family emergency--either a death in the family, an illness, a mix-up at the social security office while attempting to get her child support money, you name it. The list of troubles went on forever. It was almost comical what story she would come up with next. Pete and I had a bet going on whether she'd ever use the same person twice. I won! Her mom died twice from the time we started tracking her excuses.

To make the story worse, and to show just how bad an operation we were running, is the fact that she was one of our better-paying tenants. We figured some money was better than no money, so we allowed her to continue in that capacity. We just kept convincing ourselves, "Once we get past this next maintenance emergency or major tenant drama, we should be good." Well, that day never came. We were finally pushed to our boiling point when that tenant skipped town.

After two months of not paying rent, she simply disappeared. We went through the standard eviction process and won the right to legally regain possession of the premises. That took about forty-five days. We didn't win because we had a compelling case. We were no Matlocks. We were more like Barney Fife (I hate to say that, I'm dating myself here). Rather, we won because the defendant didn't show up in court. It was a "win" by default case. All we had to do was stand there and breathe.

Now that we had legal possession of the rental unit, our task was to assess the property and see what needed to be done to get it rent-ready again. This was always a "hold your breath and hope" moment for us to see how badly our tenants treated our "passive income investments." Many times as I stated in an earlier chapter, if we were not there quickly to secure our property, the neighbors would find their way into the home and take souvenirs such as appliances, ceiling fans, electrical wiring, our dear air conditioning units, and more. Of course, that's assuming the tenant didn't already take them as parting gifts on their way out the door.

I remember the time the next door neighbor took plants from the front of our rental house. We walked up and saw the unfilled holes where the plants had been. The neighbor coincidentally had new shrubs that looked identical to the ones we had. I asked the neighbor if he took our shrubs and, of course, he denied it. I showed him where our plants had been and pointed out the new shrubs in the front of his house. He was an older gentleman and said, "Son, you can put them back in your yard, but when you leave, I'm just going to take them again." I had to at least respect his honesty and determination. At the end of the day, he was right. He would just take them again, and with all the other battles I had raging at the time, this was not a fight I needed. I said, "Fair enough. Enjoy the plants." So Pete and I decided to put in gravel and make the unfilled hole look like a desert scene.

When we got into the property, we found that the neighbors did not "borrow" anything from the home. That was the good news. The bad news was, the tenant who was living there still had belongings inside the house. In fact, we concluded aliens must have extracted her from the premises because it looked like she was still living there. There were pictures of family events on the walls, photo albums of weddings, clothes in a fully stocked closet, and dirty dishes in the sink. Plus, she had a refrigerator full of food. There was so much stuff in there we scratched our heads wondering how she ever fit it all into a two-bedroom, two-bath 1,000-square-foot house. We were left holding a 1,000-square-foot bag and trying to figure out what to do with all of her stuff.

How we knew she was not still living in the property is the power had been shut off for over a month. We had to call the electric company to check the meter and tell us that.

Pete was in charge of the IT security division of a large department store chain and had to take an unpaid day off from work to deal with this situation. Myself being an airline pilot, I had just landed a plane with several hundred passengers and drove directly to the house still in my pilot's uniform. It must have been clear to anyone watching that we did not fit into that community. Either we were there to buy drugs, we were undercover police officers (for the record, a pilot uniform does not scream "undercover cop"), or we were two landlords that had no idea what they were doing and were about to get schooled in the ghetto yet again. Which one do you think we were?

You guessed it, if you were unsure, the school bell was about to ring.

We were short on money and decided, in our infinite wisdom, to clear the home of its contents ourselves. In the real estate world, this is called a "trash out." We wanted to ensure the make-ready crew didn't charge us for this part of the job. Since neither Pete nor myself could swing a hammer without one of us ending up in the emergency room, this was essentially the only way we could contribute to saving on expenses, Manual labor was our only practical skill.

Pete and I changed clothes in the middle of the street and stood there wearing our regular street attire. If anyone had any suspicion that we were police officers, at this point it was clear that we were not.

In ghetto neighborhoods, not many people work during the day. Most of the local people on the street knew who we were since we owned several homes there, and I'm sure they thought it was funny watching this whole thing transpire. Five hours later, after fighting off the thousands of cockroaches traversing the items we were removing, we succeeded in getting everything out of the house.

When we were done removing the refrigerator, Pete threw up. I remember it like it was yesterday. Some of the remnants of the foodstuff left in that fridge ended up on Pete, which is likely what caused his nausea. The mold and mildew was so bad there were things in that fridge we wouldn't touch. At the end of the day, we had to pay a neighborhood guy to haul it all to the dump.

We were still budget-conscious. To cut down on the number of loads the trash guy had to take, we would set items out at the curb and let the community know they could take what they wanted. We were their entertainment, and several people stopped drinking their forty ounce beers long enough to scope out the piles and search for hidden treasures.

Pete was just as upset with me as he was the situation. It wasn't because he smelled like trash and two-month old food stains either. It was something I said that set him off.

The comment exemplified that as our low-point. We had hit bottom and both of us knew it. I will never forget this. As we stood in the middle of the street stripped out of our terrible smelling street clothes so we could drop them in garbage bags and toss them to never see them again, I looked at Pete and said, "How much money do you think we saved by doing this ourselves?"

I'm not sure if it was the timing or the look of smug achievement I had on my face, but Pete let me have it. In my defense, until that moment, I thought we were doing the right thing.

Pete looked at me, picked a handful of trash off his chest, and said "Steve, you're an airline pilot. How much money do you make per hour?" Before I could answer, he continued, "I am in charge of a whole IT division. I know what I make per hour."

As I contemplated what he was trying to say, he dropped the bomb.

"Do you realize that, after paying the trash hauler guy, we saved a whopping $300? We are either going to fix this bullshit or we are selling everything we own. I will never spend my time doing this again." And Pete got in his car and drove off, leaving me in the middle of the street holding a trash bag full of stinky clothes.

I watched the neighbors rummage through the old tenant's belongings like it was Christmas. When it finally sunk in, I realized he was right. What the hell was I doing? I had such "I can do it" tunnel vision, raking around in the weeds, wracked with fear of failure, that I lost sight of the big picture. I had forgotten why I became a real estate investor in the first place.

Rising From the Ashes

Pete and I decided to try something different. We were in full-throttle fight-or-flight mode. It took awhile, but once we hit upon the winning solution, we could see the light at the end of the tunnel. The low point brought us to the place to where we could see it.

I felt like the tail we had been chasing was no longer going to be the story of our lives. Standing in the street with a trash bag full of my own dirty clothes gave me rocket fuel to make actual changes that were going to make a difference in our business. Either we were going to solve the problems we had created for ourselves, or we were going to hand them off to someone else and make them their problems.

It took awhile, but we formulated a plan. That was good because we had never had one of those.

We knew the right thing to do. We had run an apartment complex, so knowing the challenges was quite familiar to us. We just hadn't been acting like we knew what to do. That was one problem.

We took a look at the situation and decided we had three options:

First, hand our entire portfolio over to a management company. This would take the responsibility of day-to-day operations out of our hands. Since we were emotionally tied to those properties, reacting on feelings instead of running it like it was a business, this seemed like a good option.

Our second option was to establish policies and procedures, and an actual business structure, which is something we both knew we needed but clearly were not doing.

Thirdly, we could sell all our properties and walk away. The challenge that option presented was the timing. It was 2009, right when the global financial recession hit. Banks were closing their doors daily. Getting a loan on a low- income rental property wasn't going to happen. The only way an investor could buy these properties during that time was with cash. That meant we had to sell them at a loss. We weren't prepared to do that.

Since Pete had first-hand experience running the last apartment complex we owned, we decided he should be the one to interview property management companies. He interviewed several different companies over the course of two months. It was disheartening, to say the least.

He found out that no property management company wanted to manage our properties. The types of properties we owned were too time-intensive projects that (no shit) always have problem tenants. The headaches weren't worth the management fees. We realized we had a bigger problem than we first imagined.

We needed to make this work or we'd be filing bankruptcy. We weren't the dumbest people in the world even if we felt like it. But we weren't making good business decisions. We agreed right then to run our real estate investing projects like a business. We would create policies, procedures, and a structure. We'd enforce our lease agreements with the tenants. The fact that we didn't know how to do any of that never crossed our minds. We just knew it had to be done.

We started by agreeing that if tenants didn't pay their rent on time, then we were filing evictions on them and getting rid of them. There would be no negotiating or working out payment plans any more. This alone was a huge mental hurdle for us.

For me, especially. As you can imagine, when you are the one who owns the property and pays the mortgage, it can be scary to make that change, as necessary as it was.

Over the course of the next six months, we evicted seventy percent of our tenants. We invested a lot of time structuring our business like a property management company, which is the way we would want it structured if we were hiring us to manage our properties. We essentially created the foundation of our company in reverse, thinking of the customer/investor first (us) as opposed to the management company (also us) first. We were looking at it from an investor's perspective. It's important to keep in mind that, when we started, we never thought, planned, or imagined that it would be a business. At the time, it was purely for self-preservation. We wanted to keep our portfolio intact and not go bankrupt.

It's amazing how quickly things fall into place when you start treating a business like a business. Pete and I worked through many logistical challenges, going from having no structure or rules in place to having strict policies and procedures, and being constantly tested by tenants and maintenance vendors at every turn. When your back is against the wall and your whole financial existence relies on sticking to a business plan, shit starts working. After the first six months of putting the chaos behind us, we were no longer operating reactively and putting out constant fires. Nor were we running adult daycare. Deadbeat tenants who were never going to pay realized we were no longer tolerating their shenanigans. They left on their own or got a free escort out of the home by the local constable. I calculated that we evicted seventy percent of our tenants at one point during that time. Even though the properties weren't making us money, we were at least not hemorrhaging losses. Talk about restructuring. To us, that was a huge victory.

Shortly after it appeared that we had things under control, a few real estate investors from the local real estate investment clubs approached us and asked what we did to turn the corner. They wanted to know what we did to stabilize our portfolio of properties. Little did we know that many of these investors were quietly watching us, hoping we would go out of business. Their plan was to come in and buy these properties at the foreclosure sale on the courthouse steps for pennies on the dollar. They were licking their chops at our most certain demise. Had I known that I think I would have gift wrapped the keys and handed them to these investors as I drove off on several occasions. When we explained what we did to get ourselves out of our situation, you could see the heads nodding. The transformation in some of their faces was priceless. We could see they felt our pain. Truth be told, many of them had the same problems and could intimately relate to our struggles.

A few of the self-proclaimed "expert" investors called us and explained their own troubles to us. Since we had figured out how to solve our problems, they asked, "Could you manage my home for me?"

Our immediate gut reaction was, "No way, go fix your own fucking problems, like we did." Then we realized that, through economies of scale, if we wanted to keep purchasing more properties, we would some day run out of capital and other resources. Helping these other investors would be a way to produce more revenue, then we could continue to purchase properties and maybe get a volume discount from maintenance vendors and real estate agents who work with us. If we could bring them more business, then we could save money on per unit costs. So we wearily agreed to give it a try not knowing the impact that one word--"Sure"-- would have on our investing future, and our lives.

Meeting Our Coach

At that time, Pete and I owned thirty-three rental homes and Pete was part owner in a fifty-two door D-Class apartment complex. For those of you who do not know what that means, real estate investment properties are graded on a scale. The nicest and newest apartments are rated an A. As properties grow older or less desirable, their rating slides down the scale. The oldest and worst properties get a D rating.

The easiest way to explain the complex that Pete owned is to say it was on the verge of falling off the backside of that D rating. It was ridiculously bad. Located in one of the tougher parts of Houston called the Fifth Ward, it was as bad as a property could get. At the time, he still had a multi-family property management company running his apartment complex, but we figured it was just a matter of time until we brought it under the Empire umbrella.

In a very short nine months, we went from owning thirty-three homes and circling the toilet bowl of financial despair to managing thirty-three investment properties (still barely even knowing what we were doing, but at least we were taking action). And from there, we went on to manage forty-five homes owned by other investors, which made our total management portfolio add up to sixty-eight properties.

We didn't know how to manage other people's properties. We could barely manage our own. But we took on the task and brought those forty-five homes into our business structure.

Everyday, it seemed like, more people just piled their shit properties and shit problems on to us. I don't blame them, really. Why wouldn't they? It was the Greater Fool game. If they could find someone to take over their problems for them, that is a no-brainer. And because we were not thinking of this as a management business but as an investor co-op, we did it all for a flat fee of $50 per month per property. When we stopped and did the math, we were losing money. We were essentially paying them for the privilege of managing their properties and fixing their problems.

We clearly did not think it through. With our "ready, shoot, aim" mindset (me more than Pete, actually), there were some major challenges to work through.

When we had property owners asking for accounting reports on their portfolios, it was a contest to see who could be quiet the longest. Pete and I hoped they would forget the question. And, shockingly, our Jedi mind trick never seemed to work. We needed to see if there was really a business there or if we were hitting the glass ceiling of competence. Would we soon be circling another financial toilet bowl?

Pete and I were members of several local investment clubs at the time. One of them that we sponsored as a vendor called us and said they were inviting a business coach in to speak with all the sponsors. The name of the company was ActionCOACH, and she wanted to see if this coaching firm could help with our business. The investment club representative that called us said we should go to the event, and further encouraged us to sit in the front row. That was an odd request, but okay. We took them on it nonetheless.

That night, we sat and listened to this unbelievably articulate person, the lecturer's name was Mike Rager, talking about business concepts we only wished we knew. It was like he was speaking to only two people in the whole room--Pete and me. It felt like a spotlight was shining on us. This guru was telling us, "This whole speech is for you two dumbasses. Don't walk, run to sign up for our business coaching service."

ActionCOACH would ask questions like, "How long can you leave your business and let it run without you?" Leaving our business for even a few hours was a joke for Pete and me. We did everything ourselves, and we didn't do any of it well. He also discussed things like short-term and long-term goals, and asked if we had our business plan written down. Lastly, the one word that never traveled from our minds to our mouths ... "Profit." It just fell from his lips like a waterfall. Naturally.

We learned that night that the true definition of a business is a commercially profitable enterprise that runs without the owner being present. That was something we didn't have. Yet. What we owned were jobs.

That was the moment we discovered our ace in the hole. There was the guy who was going to make all the good stuff happen for us. After Mike's lecture, we waited around to talk with him and bent his ear for almost an hour telling him all of our problems. It was as if we had expected some magical answer to come out of his mouth so we could run home and plug that into the equation as the one missing piece in our business. Unfortunately, even though he told us some great things, that one word or phrase never came out. Instead, he set an appointment for us to come to his office for a diagnostic meeting. He was going to tell us what was wrong with our business.

The next week, when we got to the office, eager to hear the one word that was going to fix everything, we burned with anticipation. We were school-girl giddy and certain that we would walk out of that meeting with the magic pill that was going to skyrocket our business into orbit. Instead, he asked us a lot of questions that, unfortunately, we had zero answers for. Our hyped-up excitement morphed into a dark hole of fear and self-doubt. We felt like we would never get to where we wanted to be. Heck, we couldn't even pronounce some of the words that guy was using.

Nevertheless, we began to realize there was no magic pill. The man who diagnosed our business then introduced us to Doug Winnie, the head coach and local franchisee. He was a very nice person. He was matter of fact and straight to the point. He resonated more with Pete then myself, and we later learned why. He taught us about DISC (Dominant, Inspiring, Supportive, Cautious) personality profiles. Doug and Pete were the same profile. I was nearly polar opposite of them (a real shocker, right?).

I'll never forget sitting in Doug's office anticipating what will come next after getting a verbal beatdown from Mike Rager. We went from thinking we were going to walk out with the one word that was going to change our whole lives to wondering if we even had a business or were just wasting our time. Were we headed for another failure or getting into another mess to untangle? We had no clue.

I remember sitting on the edge of my seat waiting to hear an amazingly smart business-savvy coach give me the nod that we had a business or explain that everything we had done up to that point was for nothing. The next words out of Doug Winnie's mouth would change our lives one way or another. Either way, I'd at least have closure.

He examined our questionnaires, which were quite lengthy, and the answers we gave--and, in some cases, didn't--looked at us with his matter-of-fact skull-piercing eyes.

"The good news," he said, "is you two do, in fact, have the potential for a business. The bad news is you are nowhere near running it well enough to survive. You guys will be out of business and owing money to a lot of creditors very soon if you do not change some things."

The next sentence is what we needed to hear: "Lucky for you, I can help."

We were convinced before we walked into the meeting that if we felt he could help get this business going, then we were in. His response solidified in our heads that the right answer was to hire him. We signed up for his program on the spot. We knew that we could not afford him, but we also knew that we could not afford not to hire him. We were damned if we did and damned if we didn't. More damned if we didn't. We were not going to fail at this if there was even a sliver of possibility that we could succeed.

Burning the boats

The next few months were consumed with learning new business acronyms as we worked our way through Doug's coaching program. It was a systematic program with six steps designed to teach us how to create the proper structure for our business. Some of the acronyms he threw at us were P&L (profit and loss), COGS (cost of goods sold), and CAC (customer acquisition cost), none of which we had heard before.

The days were filled with frustration as we despaired in learning the things we had never thought of before trying to fathom how we would climb this mountain of our own making. When we did occasionally do something correctly and could see the process taking better shape, we'd get excited and hopeful. These times often included closing a client or adding another property to our business. Sometimes, it was more involved, like creating a system to help us manage the business better. Once we got a better understanding of where our little dinghy was headed, our resolve was unshakeable.

Slowly, we began to see that we really did have a business. This became so evident that at one point--on December 1, 2012--Pete took two big leaps and logged them into the Empire history books. The first of those was quitting his job. That day would be his first full-time day of running Empire. It was also a monumental day for the company because it was the day our first official full-time employee, Lisa, punched in. We met her at one of the local property manager association events and, as time went on, we would call and ask her how we should handle certain situations. She was a wealth of knowledge in the property management industry and always willing to help. Plus, she gave solid advice, which was pure gold to us at the time. She seemed to really like the fire that Pete and I had in our bellies.

We call that day "the day we burned our boats." See, in 334 AD, Alexander the Great decided to invade Persia. When they arrived, however, they discovered the Persian army was much larger than theirs. To ensure his men were committed to battle, he told them, "We are going home in Persian boats. We are not going home in our own." And he told his men to burn the boats. Alexander and his men won that battle and sailed home as victors in Persian boats. It's a lesson in zero-option mentality, and that was our thinking as we opened up this new chapter in Empire history.

Our excitement was almost contagious. When we got around investors or other property managers and talked about what we were doing, and singing the praises of our business coach, that excitement rubbed off. In the months leading up to that historic day, we asked Lisa if she could recommend someone for the position we were hiring for. Since she had been in the property management business for such a long time, we figured she'd have a name or two to drop into the hat. It shocked us when she expressed an interest in the position herself. The fact that a veteran in the business would be willing to take a chance on the two of us was awe-inspiring, to say the least.

I think our drive and passion was much more intoxicating then we realized, and the fact that we were building a good foundation with the help of our business coach put our abilities in the spotlight. Others saw them before Pete and I did. We clearly did not have much experience, besides our own failures as investors, but we made up for it in enthusiasm.

Our plan was to operate Empire out of Pete's Class-D apartment complex. This made sense to us because it would save us on office rent. Plus, Pete could be on site to keep an eye on the complex. But it also meant that Lisa would have to drive into the ghetto every day. When we told her that was going to be our office, we thought she wouldn't show up. That place was scary. It was intimidating just to look at it from the road.

When the big day came, Pete burned his boat, quit his job, and took the leap of faith. We hired a full-time property manager, purchased some computers and a safe, and opened the doors. We were all set, we thought. What could go wrong? Then the phone rang. Someone had broken into the office and stolen a bunch of equipment before the first day even started. It was as if one of our gem-like tenants was sending us a message: "Welcome to Minden Square Apartment Complex. Have a nice fucking day!"

It was a not nice day.

More Chaotic Growth

We did not let the break-in faze us. Pete and I had been through so much already that we just passed it off as a normal Monday and kept on moving. Nothing was going to stop us. We felt it was our destiny to succeed, and we were ready to get in the rink and ring the bell to start the fight.

The first few months were scary and exciting. We were committed to following the advice of our property manager, and it was nice to actually have a legitimate property manager. Lisa's first order of business was to deal with our part-time (a generous perception) helper.

As I think back on it, I think what happened is the part-time helper knew Lisa wasn't going to tolerate her taking advantage of us like Pete and I did, so she just stopped showing up. That would have been great except she was also a tenant in a separate rental property I owned. In addition to losing an employee, I was faced with evicting a tenant in the first week.

It became a long and drawn out process to get her out of the property. It took the full forty-five days and the constable forcibly removing her, but, as we agreed when we first started, Pete and I were committed to doing whatever it took. Eventually, we got her out of the property and, like a bad meal, it passed.

Our new manager's next business task was to deal with some of the clients we were managing properties for. After conducting an inventory of the homes we managed and their owners, she came to an interesting conclusion, which we didn't see coming. She told us over half of the owners were going to get us sued or fined if we didn't get rid of them.

We were managing roughly eighty properties at that time, and thirty-three of those belonged to Pete and me. Since we charged a measly $50 per month in management fees, and Pete and I were the Fifth Ward's ghetto whisperers, the types of owners we attracted were other low-end property owners and cheap landlords who didn't want to pay what it was actually worth to manage their properties. It was the perfect recipe for a headache, heartburn, and high-octane stress. Lisa was not about to let the worse-case scenario happen to us.

She promptly fired half of the owners whose properties we managed and put the rest on notice. What was funny, and also sad, was that we were then Empire's biggest client. She told them Empire was going to start doing things the right way and this was not a place where they could do whatever they wanted and get away with it. They were not going to put our company in jeopardy. Needless to say, that was scary but necessary. Pete and I finally had someone to answer to who was looking out for our best interests. I could not just go out and sign up any owner and promise them the world just to get their business.

We continued our chaotic growth for the next eighteen months. We hired people, adding to the staff, and did everything our business coach told us to do. We were paying him a lot of money, so why not listen to him? Shockingly, we were in the minority with this type of thinking. He told us many people pay a lot of money for coaching and continue to do it their own way. That type of thinking doesn't make sense to me.

Pete and I were still having cash flow problems, and we had to make a big business decision. It was time to raise our prices.

The way our prices were structured, we couldn't hire more staff. In order to sustain the growth we were experiencing, we needed money to reinvest back into the company. After much deliberation, and several exercises in mental gymnastics, we raised our rates to ten percent of property rent for new clients and $75 for a few grandfathered clients.

It was a scary thing for us because we kept pondering the pertinent questions, like how much to raise them, and when is the right time to raise them? We were afraid we would lose some of our property owners as clients. But our coach told us to do it, so we raised the rates. And, it shocked us, but there was very little push back from any of our clients. We thought the world would implode just by talking about raising rates. We were sure we'd have no clients left. In reality, there was no cheaper pricing on the market, so where were they going to go? It was time for us to stop paying them to manage their properties, and we did.

There were a few property owners who ditched us. Those were the cheap ones, the ones with really bad properties, or just simply bad owners. They pretty much fired themselves. Our cleansing had begun, and it started to feel good. Raising our rates created more revenue because the new owners we signed up were at higher rates and were better clients who didn't require as much of our management time.

The Culture and Surroundings

It's interesting what becomes normal when you are exposed to something day in and day out and don't know any better.

Remember Pete's D-grade apartment complex? We had our management office on that property. Where do you think people would come for maintenance issues, rent payments, and to solve their domestic problems? Right there to our office. And, of course, there were the police raids that would sometimes sweep through the complex, as common as fair weather in Texas. Oddly enough, that became our norm. We were so focused on growing Empire that apartment complex became a stepping stone to our success.

Pete and I eventually took over managing that apartment complex. It was a natural progression since we were there everyday and had the best possible set of eyes on it (Lisa), as opposed to an offsite management company that never stepped foot on the property. Since Pete was part owner and had a vested interest in the property, he could make sure it was looked after properly.

One day, something not quite so normal happened. I rode to work on my motorcycle, and there was a horse tied to the fence. Contrary to what some people think, not everyone in Houston rides horses. Certainly not in the city, and definitely not in the ghetto streets of the Fifth Ward. I parked next to the horse. We exchanged furtive glances and I laughed, shaking my head in disbelief. I walked into the office and no one, including myself, mentioned the horse tied to the fence in our parking lot. I said to myself, one day I'm going to write a book about all this. To this day, no one knows whose horse that was.

After a year of coaching, we were beginning to see some great results from our business. Our business coach came to the office to see what kind of environment we had to work in. He wanted to get a better look at our company culture. We were meeting with him for one hour a week, so he was aware of the challenges we had operating out of the apartment complex. Or so we thought. After coming to our office and almost getting his new Lexus tires stolen off his car, he promptly explained that we needed to get out of there as soon as possible. We needed to change our environment fast.

Pete and I were so focused on doing the job at hand, we never realized how our environment was affecting our employees as well the types of clients we would attract. We were swimming in a pool of poison and never realized it.

We didn't know it at the time, but that was why we had such a high employee turnover. And that doesn't account for the numerous potential employees who didn't show up for interviews. Within two months, we had moved from a D-class ghetto apartment complex in the Fifth Ward of Houston to an A-class building in one of the best areas of Houston. Not only did this place have an elevator, but it had a door man where you had to sign in. We had onsite security! Things were changing at Empire.

Time to Cut the Cancer and Leave the Ghetto

Empire continued to grow by leaps and bounds. Pete and I continued to struggle with our own low-end properties. As hard as we tried, we couldn't figure out a successful business model with those types of properties. We stopped taking on clients with low-income homes. As a matter of fact, we ended up being Empire's biggest low-income client. We could never figure out how to keep tenants from leaving while enforcing our lease agreements.

It was a constant seesaw. Every time we enforced our lease agreement with late fees or refused to fix non-required maintenance items, a tenant would leave. If that wasn't the challenge, then we were paying three times the average maintenance cost on required maintenance items simply because the homes were so old. We could not turn a profit.

Finally, one day, as we were discussing the latest rounds of issues with our personal properties, Pete said, "We need to sell these things. We need to cut out the cancer. They're killing us."

Once we came to this conclusion, it was as if a huge weight had been lifted off our shoulders and we could see the light at the end of this dark tunnel we had dug ourselves into. The solution had been sitting in front of us the whole time. The thought of selling them instantly made me feel better. I could see a way out of the tunnel.

Pete and I knew we could buy more properties in the future, but focusing on the growth of Empire was our main priority. It wasn't dealing with ghetto homes that were not returning any profits, and more importantly, taking up valuable time.

One of the reasons those properties did not make sense for us, from a business management perspective, is because the number of employee staff hours it took to manage properties below a certain price point was almost double than for mid-priced rental homes. Property management company fee structures are based on a percentage amount of rent collections. Anything below the price point meant we were doing more work for less money, and taking a loss. That included our own properties. Owning these low-end properties was distracting us from our core business focus of growing the property management business.

So we put our heads together and laid out a plan. The real estate industry was still reeling from the global financial recession, so banks weren't giving out loans freely. And these homes had no appreciation, meaning we had virtually no equity built into them.

One option we had was to sell them to other investors for the price that we bought them for. If we were lucky, we might get a little more. But the money we put into them for make readies, maintenance, and capital improvements would be wiped away clean and taken as losses. The interesting thing is, we were so fed up and mentally exhausted from the constant drama that came with those properties that we were fine with losing that money. As a matter of fact, when we did sell them, there were several closings that we paid the closing costs just to get the deal done. I think we were the happiest ones in the room even though we had to bring a check to pay the difference between what we owed on the property and what we sold it for.

These properties were no longer going to be our problem. Those problems were soon to belong to someone else. And make no mistake, these investors knew what they were getting. We did, and still do, believe that these homes were great investments with the right business model even if we couldn't figure out what that model is. They simply did not align with our business plans and were becoming a distraction to us achieving our goals.

Pete's main focus over the next year was to sell those properties. We sold all thirty-three properties we owned except for a handful that we decided we would keep. We got creative in selling them too. We sold to end buyers at full price and investors at steep discounts, and there were a few that we sold to investors where we carried the financing (basically, we were the bank). On top of that, we put in the sales agreement that Empire would continue to manage the property.

It took us a year-and-a-half to get these properties unloaded, but we were the happiest we could be when we sold our last property. We were then able to laser-focus on growing Empire with no distractions.

Some of the owners who hung onto these properties did go through a re-gentrification period, and some of these properties are worth a lot more money now than when we owned them. That's real estate. If you know the trends and see the indicators, you can receive some handsome rewards. We just could not hold on to that many bad properties for that long.

For our sanity, and desire to rid ourselves of these headaches, we got out of these deals because we wanted to focus our money, time, and attention on growing Empire. And to be honest, it didn't matter to us that these problems were no longer ours.

Welcome to NARPM

As Pete and I learned more about the property management industry, we became aware of the National Association of Residential Property Managers, commonly referred to as NARPM. This national non-profit organization helps fellow property managers obtain a place to meet, discuss best practices, discuss industry challenges, and more. One of the key benefits of being a member is being able to network with other property managers and discuss common challenges. Property management companies, big and small, new and old, all talk freely and help each other solve critical issues. Without NARPM, our company would not look like it does today.

When Pete and I hired Lisa Porterfield, we met her at one of NARPM's luncheons. Fate had us sitting next to each other and exchanging business cards. That was an important day for us because she helped us solve a lot of problems.

NARPM meetings were full of operators sharing tidbits of information and letting us know of things that were not such good ideas. Another way of putting it is to say certain practices are "frowned upon" by governing agencies. As a result, our business grew and became more efficient.

Pete is the integrator. He is a systems- and structure-oriented kind of guy. That means he really knows how to connect with people in this group. He later became the Houston chapter president and as, of this writing, he is regional vice president for the Central United States chapters. While in the chapter president role, he grew the membership and vendor sponsorship of the Houston chapter to levels it had never seen before. He simply used the knowledge we had been learning from Doug Winnie and applied it to growing the business of NARPM, putting his systems approach to work for the organization.

Pete did so much that year as president that he won the coveted "Rocky Maxwell Award," which is an award given by the national NARPM to the rookie of the year. Getting that award elevated him as someone to keep an eye on, and it also put Empire Industries on the map. I can say the personal and business relationships we have made through this organization have paid us back many times over. Plus, we've made many lifelong friends. One person in particular, Eric Wetherington, gave us an amazing amount of help through sheer generosity, and I will never forget it.

Why Reinvent the Wheel? Ask the Experts for Help

The more involved we got in NARPM, the more Pete and I learned that we were doing some things fundamentally wrong. We had systems in place that were dependent on a single person and therefore not scalable. There were better practices that we could have implemented. It seemed like a tidal wave of information every time we went to an event and heard someone talk about a subject related to our business. One day, while we were discussing the latest information dump, we came up with the bright idea of calling one of these gargantuan, mythic property management companies and asking if we could visit their office to see how they run their operation. Why reinvent the wheel? If there were people out there doing it better than we were, why not learn from them?

We picked a company that was not geographically close to us. In fact, it wasn't even in Texas. That way, competition would not be a factor, and the size of our company dwarfed in comparison to theirs. It was inconceivable to us that our company would grow to their size. All we wanted to do is look under the hood. That's why we chose to call Eric Wetherington of CarolinaOne Property Management in South Carolina.

An interesting lesson we learned early on is the value of talking to the right people about our business. When we spoke to other investors about our business ideas, some of them would tell us all the reasons why those ideas wouldn't work. They would tell us the wrong things just to make us fail. It became a colossal waste of time and energy for us to share what we were thinking with some people. I remember hearing more than once, "What works in one market won't work in another." We learned who the true business people were.

Some of the more successful business owners told us it was a smart move to visit another property management firm and learn from them. We were shocked when we called Eric and he happily agreed. He said he would love for us to spend the day observing his operation from the inside.

This was a true testament to NARPM and how members are willing to help other members. Pete and I scheduled a day and excitedly planned for the trip. At the time, we had roughly one hundred eighty properties, so the challenges we had were very different than the ones CarolinaOne was dealing with. We honestly didn't know what challenges lurked around the corner for us because they didn't even exist yet. To our amazement, we showed up to this huge building full of employees. The parking lot was full of vehicles with company logos on them. We were in awe. After giving us a tour of the building and introducing us to all the different departments of his company, Eric Wetherington sat down with us in his large, exquisite conference room for what we thought was going to be a cozy little chat. But something amazing happened.

One by one, he brought in each department head and had them explain what their role and job description was, and what they were accountable for. After that, we were allowed to ask them questions. This went on all day.

Pete and I left there with about twenty pages of notes each and a much clearer vision of the future direction of Empire. We agreed that if anyone ever wanted to see our operation, we would be happy to pay it forward. The most amazing thing I remember about that day was our host sitting in the room with us answering our questions the entire time. He had to be a busy man, but he took the time to meet with us. How in the world could he just disconnect from running his company to sit with us all day? Later, I realized that is the difference between you running your business or your business running you. He had a business that ran without him. Funny how this points back to the definition of a business we learned when we first met our business coach.

Agent Alliance Program

After our trip, Pete and I tried our best to break down some of the things we could implement immediately and choose what were going to be bigger projects to focus on for the future. One thing we both zeroed in on were successful programs

CarolinaOne implemented that was directly attributed to their growth. Because Pete and I think differently, we both took away different things. He took away more structural and procedural concepts that would help the company run more smoothly, and I focused more on the marketing and sales ideas. One of the marketing concepts I took away was something completely new to me. Here's the idea: Use in-house real estate agents as a referral source to attract investor clients. That was a great idea if we had any agents. Since we didn't, we had a bit of a challenge.

What we did have was fire and energy. After visiting with Eric, we developed an end goal, a destination. We knew what we wanted our company to look like.

Since we didn't have any real estate agents working under us, we did the next best thing. I drove to a local real estate broker's office and explained how they could work with us as a preferred property management company, and we would become their strategic partner. Of course, selling this concept was not that easy. We soon learned property management companies and real estate agents mix like oil and vinegar.

The reason is quite simple. In my opinion, it all comes down to greed, lack of planning, and setting expectations. Many real estate agents believe if they refer a client to a property management company, they will lose that client for any future real estate deals. To be honest, it's not just a perception. It's a reality. So, for the record, I can understand their frustration. But what I could not understand was why they weren't trying to figure out a solution to this million-dollar problem. In their minds, they would rather not have a property management company to refer to so that they will never lose any potential future sales. At the same time, they missed out on a lot of potential future business.

The average investor owns three to five investment properties. The average retail buyer purchases two houses in their lifetime. But here's an interesting fact: When an investor buys their first property, they do not use the real estate agent that helped them buy their personal home. Why? Because it is not even in the agent's mindset to ask for that business. They are so turned off by the idea of the investor world that they let business they have already paid to acquire go to another agent. And they're not just losing one deal to that agent, but multiple investment property deals.

Many agents have the mindset that an investor is this super-sophisticated person who wants deals at fifty percent of the value, is intimidating, and is a waste of their time. While these types of investors do exist, they are the minority. The reality is, investors are people who usually have careers, but they want a more secure retirement. They're looking for higher returns than they might get with their 401Ks or IRAs. Eighty percent of real estate investments are done by first-time investors. At least, that's the number I've heard.

The numbers are staggering on purchases and sales for repeat business. If real estate agents could figure out a way to solve that problem, in my opinion, they would increase their business substantially with little work.

After numerous meetings with real estate agents and being rejected several times, we came up with an idea. What if we were able to pay the agent a monthly referral fee every month, but if their client ever decided to sell the property that we managed, then we would guarantee that we referred the client back to the agent so they have the sale?

We asked that question of a few real estate agents and the response was overwhelming.

"I can get paid a referral fee on a monthly basis and you'll give the client back to me for the sale? Not only will I give you all of my business, but I will refer you out to other real estate agents I know!"

That's how we knew we were onto something.

Shortly thereafter, we started coming up with all of the reasons real estate agents should not be involved in property management. What we found out was that one out of three real estate investors are involved in some form of litigation or legal violation every year. Secondly, real estate agents are considered professionals because they hold a license, so they are held to a higher standard. They could face fines, violations by the state real estate commission, and possible revocation of their license if they aren't careful. In doing our due diligence, we found that a lot of real estate offices don't allow their agents to manage properties because it's such a huge liability.

Many brokerages have liability insurance if they are doing property management. But unless property management is done at a large volume, it doesn't make financial sense for them. Because they don't do property management, a lot of the real estate agents will shy away from investors. Again, what the agent and the broker have failed to realize is that the average investor owns anywhere between three and five properties. They sell those properties on years three, five, or seven, statistically. What that means is, brokers are losing a lot of potential revenue from purchases, sales, and leasing, all because real estate agents do not deal with investors. There was something here and we were close to figuring it out.

Talking to brokers and seeing them understand how much revenue they're leaving on the table by not working with a certain type of clientele made them realize they needed to figure out a solution to that problem. As luck would have it, we came in as the solution. We offered a completely separate entity, a professional property management company that their agents could use to refer their clients to. It gave them the ability to understand investing more while helping their investor clients work with a reputable company. This gave brokerages liability release without having to worry about litigation. It would lead to more purchases and more sales for the brokerage and more property management clients for us to manage. We hit upon a win/win solution.

For the next two years, we set off doing nothing but constant door knocking on real estate offices. I think we must have delivered over a thousand sandwiches to hungry agents just so they would listen to us pitch our company. Of course, the first reaction to a property management company walking into their office was not positive. It was like walking into a lion's den. We took food with us so it took the edge off. Then we could explain to them what our business model was and how it was completely different than what they were used to. We called it the "Agent Alliance 20/20 Program."

What that meant was, if an agent referred a client to us, then we would pay that agent twenty percent commission every month for the first year as a referral fee. If the owner wanted to sell their property, they would get the sale referred back to the agent. The other twenty percent of our 20/20 plan came from the leasing of the property. If the agent wanted to be the leasing agent, we were okay with that. However, some agents prefer to focus on the sales part of the deal instead of the leasing. If the agent did not want to lease the property, then we would lease the property and pay the agent a twenty percent referral fee.

After the program started getting traction, more agents referred their clients to us. So we took it a step further. In order to make sure that we protected our coveted one percent eviction rate, we decided to perform the credit criminal background checks free of charge for brokers and do them in-house. That got the real estate agent off the hook on performing those background checks. Since we leased so many properties on a regular basis, it was not difficult for us to do the credit criminal background check. We already had a system in place to do that. Also, by doing it that way, we could ensure that we placed a qualified tenant that met our standards in a unit and standardize our procedures.

Agents don't perform those background checks very often, so it's a weakness of theirs. We tracked the difference between us placing a tenant through our background checks and an agent placing a tenant and found that, statistically, we would evict more tenants that were placed by outside real estate agents than if we did the background check and accepted or denied the tenant based on our criteria. In the end, we did not have to evict as many tenants when we performed and selected them based on our criteria, which ultimately gave the owner a more reasonable and stable investment property with less headaches. That was the reason they hired us in the first place.

Our program was so successful that, in 2015, we won the Business Excellence Award for "Best Marketing in North America" from ActionCOACH. We had a 1,471% return on our marketing dollars because of our Agent Alliance Program. We also became the highest referred property management company in Houston because we paid out more referral fees to real estate agents than any other property management company. By synergistically partnering with them, by us working on the abundance theory and giving up the sale, we picked up a lot of clients and made up for it in volume. We also turned real estate agents into raving fans and paid them well for the referrals they sent us. It did take quite a while to get our momentum wheel turning with this program, but once we did, it clearly became our number one source of leads.

Chapter 3

Creating the Empire Brand

We learned early on that if we were going to grow our company, then we had to learn about branding, and we needed to have a clear focus on marketing. One of the first employees we hired was a marketing specialist, Kevin Davidson, to help us brand our company. We wanted to make sure we were getting the Empire name out on as many online and physical real-world platforms as possible, and to make sure we were a force to be reckoned with among investors and real estate agents. We wanted people to know who we were.

We were not marketing experts by any stretch of imagination, and, to be completely honest, we didn't anticipate the growth that was in store for us. We didn't even understand the factors that would drive that growth. However, we knew we had a good product. We had a lot of interest in what we were doing, and we also knew we needed to hire someone who knew how to market a business with little to no capital.

We found our man in Kevin, front and center. I knew the first day he showed up for the interview. He was the first one there and had the most professional attitude we had yet to meet. He knew nothing about real estate or the property management business, but, then again, we knew nothing about marketing.

"You're hired!"

We learned early on that marketing is not an expense. It's an investment in the company. Another way of saying that: Businesses don't spend money on marketing; they invest money in marketing, and we took it from that approach starting at day one. We made sure we had a budget (as small as it was), and we spent every dollar of that budget on marketing. We constantly tried to find ways to squeeze a little more out of each dollar.

In the beginning, it was just Kevin and me. We would throw ideas against the wall just to see which ones would stick. Our many brainstorming sessions gave us plenty of fodder.

Learning to Speak Well

As Empire started to mature as a company, I began to schedule more speaking events around town at any venue that would allow me to speak. It became a part of our marketing strategy. It wasn't long before I realized that I really enjoyed public speaking. I enjoyed making a connection with my audience. However, when I stepped in front of larger crowds, I got much more nervous, which diminished how well I connected with the audience.

My first time out helped me understand better why public speaking is the biggest fear most people have, even more than death. Oddly enough, I could see why. It was one of the hardest things I'd ever do, but I was not going to back down from the challenge. I made up my mind, I was going to conquer my fear and step on its throat when I won the battle.

To get over the fear of public speaking, I read a lot of books, and took some classes on public speaking so that I'd learn to be more comfortable in my own skin while standing on stage feeling hundreds of eyes burning through me. I knew the content well, but I felt like some people were judging me as a phony or a fake. At least, that's what went through my brain while I was speaking.

Instead, what typically happened is those people I thought were judging me were the ones who would thank me afterward. Many of them told me I moved them, and they were focused entirely on what I was saying. It's all about perception, and perspective.

I will never forget, years later, one guy at a keynote presentation I gave. He looked as if I ran over his dog on the way to the venue that day. His eyes burned through my soul, and, for some reason, I couldn't stop looking at him. It reminded me of a car wreck on the side of the freeway where, out of curiosity, all the drivers slow down and stare. After an hour of playing this eye-fuck game, I could feel myself getting upset at him. I thought, "Who is this guy? Does he think he's better than me? He doesn't even know me. Fuck him!"

After the event, several people came up to thank me for giving the speech. When I turned around, I was nose to nose with this guy. It was as if time had slowed down and Brad Pitt from Fight Club had jumped from the crowd to launch a melee right there. But the polar opposite happened. He wrapped his arms around me, gave me the biggest bear hug I've ever had, and thanked me for moving him so deeply. He said, "I felt like you were talking only to me, and you knew my story because your story was similar to mine. Now, I do not feel alone in my fight to be a better person. Thank you from the bottom of my heart."

After that day, I've never had that feeling about anyone in the crowd, and it just goes to show that you never know how you can move people with your message.

To become better at public speaking, and to achieve Empire's goal of becoming the top Realtor-referred property management company in Houston, I'd speak or teach classes at three or four real estate offices per week. I'd speak even if they only gave me five minutes. I'd try to stretch it to seven or ten minutes, if I could. What could they do? Not let me speak again? I had one shot to make a first impression, and that was enough time to spark an interest. It wasn't, however, enough time for them to ask questions that I may or may not have been able to answer. Realtor referrals soon became our number one marketing strategy and source of new leads. We decided we needed to get more focused on content.

First, we wanted to make sure agents returned again and again to hear me speak, and we wanted them to view us as experts. Secondly, we wanted them to refer their clients to us. In order for this to happen, they have to first know you, like you, and trust you.

We created a list of multiple topics that I would speak on. It didn't take long to develop four to five different educational topics for real estate agents, and I'd talk about those at my lunch and learning classes. But real estate agents don't typically work in the office, and they are considered contract workers so they couldn't be forced to attend a lesson. That made it difficult to get them there, and I needed to find ways to keep it interesting so they'd want to hear me speak. That also allowed me to inform them of our amazing referral program. If we tried to push our program without valuable content, we'd be seen just like everyone else and not win on the trust factor. I learned that if I had a certified education class for Realtors, it would increase attendance.

As licensed Realtors, they are required by the Texas Real Estate Commission (TREC) to take mandatory recurrent education classes to keep their license certification status. By becoming a certified instructor, I'd attract more attendance to my classes. When I learned that, I immediately got certified to teach Continuing Education courses for real estate agents in Texas. That meant I was speaking as an education authority and not just a property management company representative trying to get their business.

This marketing strategy proved to be successful, but it couldn't be our only marketing channel. In order for us to obtain our goals, we needed to maintain momentum on multiple marketing fronts. That was when digital marketing was beginning to take on more importance in real estate. Several online marketing gurus told me I needed to have a lot of content on my website to get on the front page of Google. At the time, video content was king of the hill. So I accepted that challenge with the same tenacity I had with everything else.

The first thing we did was hire a social media company. They told me I needed ten videos within two weeks. Knowing most people might complete one or two, the gurus try to push people out of their comfort zone. I'm not like most people. I smashed out fifty videos in two weeks.

The social media gurus couldn't believe it. They thought I had a bunch of video content saved up or was using the same material over and over again. They were wrong on both fronts. Step on the throat and win at all costs, that was my motto.

Next, they said we needed to focus on online reputation management reviews. Within a month, I had thirty reviews on Google.

Within a short period of time, we eclipsed that number. We ended up getting eighty online Google reviews and were uploading videos all over the internet. Those videos got me even more comfortable with public speaking. Soon, I was consistently creating two to three videos of solid content every single week on different topics that were relevant to real estate investors and their pain points.

All of those videos and reviews garnered a lot of attention for us in the property management industry. We began noticing people talking about us. Some were asking if we were the guys making the videos and others wanted to know how we got so many reviews. At that point, we knew we were onto something and were not letting off the gas for one second. It was time for fifth gear.

As our marketing and branding strategies continued, people asked if I would be a guest on their radio show or podcast. I accepted all offers and the invitations increased. I became a "yes man" to any offer. The show hosts really seemed to be interested in my story of transitioning from airline pilot to failed investor to successful entrepreneur. It became a point of interest in how the direct effect of 9/11 caused the creation of one of the fastest growing property management companies in Houston.

All of that attention made me think some larger show hosts might want me on their shows, so I started sending emails out to some of the biggest radio shows and real estate podcasts at the time. I'd hound them like I did when trying to get my first airline job, asking over and over again if I could be on the show. Because it was a post-9/11 feel good story, the hosts liked it from a business sense. In reality, all I wanted to do was get on the radio and learn to become a better speaker, and to get the Empire name out there. I wish I could say I had a sophisticated goal, but my goal was really nothing more than massive execution.

I enjoyed being a guest on the various shows and connected with people very easily. When I'd speak, I had the ability to talk real estate, business, and airplanes. The conversations took many turns based on the host's interest in my topic. On one show, we talked about the hydraulic and electrical system of the Boeing 787, and what my scariest flying moments were. After that, I was approached by the producer of a TV reality series who said to me, "For someone who looks like a member of a motorcycle gang, or a professional wrestler, you sure know how to articulate well." As funny as that was, I was in for whatever they wanted to throw at me. I even created some sizzle reels and sent them as auditions for a potential show series of my own, but I'm still waiting to hear back on those. Who knows when I'll get the call to be the next Steve Harvey, or The Rock?

It doesn't matter, I'm in.

Gaining Traction Through Marketing

I found my footing in this new environment by slowly and steadily separating myself from the pack of standard property management company owners. To me, it was obvious why I never imagined myself as a property manager. I owned a business. It just so happened that the business I owned was a property management company. That was the ultimate mindset difference. I was later told it was a subconscious paradigm shift. I did it without consciously knowing about it.

Don't get me wrong. There are some great owner-operators in this industry, and they really love property management. For me, I was operating in the beginning phase of a new company creation. Property management was simply a business category.

Pete and I getting our heads smashed in once a week by our business coach taught me a few lessons about business. The first of these is that businesses--all businesses--operate under the same structural chassis. Marketing makes the phone ring while sales answers the phone and converts leads to customers. How many times you persuade each customer to buy from you produces a total amount of transactions. Based on how much you charge for products or services, that leads to revenue. Revenue minus expenses equals profit margin. Simple, but it makes sense.

When I learned that lesson for the first time, I left a puddle of drool on the table. My eyes locked in on the chart in front of me. It so nicely illustrated a simple truth of business. I remember thinking, What the hell does this have to do with me wanting a rental property in case another 9/11 tragedy happened again?

But on the other side of the learning curve, things became much more clear. I learned what my role in the business would be. As my excitement and passion to learn more about business grew, I realized we needed to have a bigger presence online, especially social media. I spoke to everyone I could find who might be considered a "social media expert." I thought these self-proclaimed gurus had the magic pill to get us to the coveted number on spot on Google. Every one of them told me what the other companies were doing wrong and how they could fix it. Some of them claimed to have an inside contact at Google, or they fed me some other load of crap. All I got was a load of empty promises. Unfortunately, not much else materialized.

Empire went through so many different social media "experts" that all seemed to say the right things but could never deliver on their promises because of some reason out of their control. I kept thinking, No shit it's out of your control, but isn't that why I hired you? All I wanted was to be on page one of Google. Why was that so hard?

While tearing through social media rejects, the one thing I did consistently was pick their brains as much as possible. Through Q & A strategy sessions, I was able to piece together a long-term social media strategy on my own.

I noticed there were some things all the gurus agreed on. It was that I needed to create as much online content as possible, and it should come in the form of video. Each time I heard one of these suggestions, I took that as real solid information. I viewed their failures as paying for my lessons in marketing. Their inability to deliver on their promises was my gain.

The biggest piece of gold I gleaned from the one company I first hired and still I am good friends with to this day is that I needed to present myself as an educator and not just someone selling a product or service. That little nugget of knowledge is worth way more than the price of this book (assuming you purchased it).

Empire needed to provide a solution to our target client's problems. The implied task there is figuring out what those problems are.

As I have learned from continual reading is that most companies sell solutions to problems as they perceive it while customers buy products and services that fix their problems. Unfortunately, these are often not the same thing. That was one of the reasons Empire was on the back page of Google (Page 59, to be exact). We weren't selling a solution to anyone's problem.

In case you're wondering. For the record, I didn't know Google had that many pages for their search queries. What searcher would even care at that point? More importantly, we started to understand the reason we were so far back in the rankings was this little thing called search engine optimization (SEO, for short). We had multiple SEO issues, one of which is that our website was thin on the content and that led to low web page traffic.

One common reason people visit a website is the content. When you have a bunch of online videos, you have what few other people are willing to have: effective online content. It's like a library for the average investor who is looking to solve a problem. Good content solves a problem they have, or points the way to a solution. Since we had no content, we had no solutions. Therefore, no website traffic. Basically, we sucked.

We learned that Google likes video content for SEO purposes, and if you wanted to rank organically on Google, then you better get in front of the camera. This meant that I needed to learn how to do video blogs, and to do them in a way that answers questions and solves problems. Otherwise, no one would watch our videos, which would put me back to where I was in Google (page 59). Producing a bunch of video content helped us in our quest to land on page one of Google's search results.

As I stated earlier the first company we hired explained that more videos was better. When we hired them, we signed up for a package of ten video blogs, with their help and guidance. That was all that I needed to light the fire in my belly. Within a two weeks, I had over fifty videos, and I never slowed down or looked back. To this day, I create two to five videos per week in order to keep our search rankings up.

One other thing I was told was that reputation management held the keys to our online success. Again, after hearing it from multiple people, and being someone that will always buy from the company that has more positive reviews than everyone else, this made sense to me. Online reviews are viewed as personal referrals in that they establish Know, Like, and Trust in the sales cycle.

Bam! I was off to the races. I'd asked everyone I ever worked with, talked to, answered a question for, or even knew, for an online review. To this day, it amazes me that a genuine request for help will elicit a positive response from most people. I will admit, I felt a little guilty sometimes (much like the guilt trips my Jewish mom takes me on when I don't call her often enough), but I was on a mission and nothing was going to slow me down, much less stop me. Step on the throat!

Empire was starting a massive movement that was gaining momentum. We were doing, quite simply, what needed to be done. As the gurus promised, we started to climb in the search engine rankings.

Our focus was simple: Ask everyone we did business with for an online review and continually provide valuable video content to answer the real questions our target clients had.

As we made this our main focus, we learned that there are "happy points" in the service industry. It has to do with the law of reciprocity. Basically, I did for you, now you do for me. It is some upper-level psychological bullshit that I will not even attempt to explain. But, essentially, anytime someone is happy and thanks you for something that you've done, it provides an opportunity to ask for something in return, such as an online review. So, for example, when you accept a tenant into a property, fix a maintenance issue for an owner or a tenant, solve a problem, get the owner their first month's rent, get an invoice lowered from a vendor, which helps the property owner, these are all times people are happy and will perform a favor in return.

It's like those very expensive drink containers that keep your iced tea cold or your coffee hot for a whole week. I don't know how, but that shit works. We did finally make it to number one on Google and, to this day, we have the most Google reviews than any of our competitors with over four hundred fifty Google reviews and over six hundred total reviews online as of this writing. This single strategy was instrumental in Empire's incredible growth.

While this was an amazing accomplishment that combined a lot of consistent hard work on many fronts, it is also a blessing and a curse. When you have a young, inexperienced company in high growth mode, someone on the back end needs to process orders and provide the promised customer experience or you can lose clients faster than you get them. We had to put together a system that prevented that from happening.

The Chaos of a Pressure Cooker Office

Because the property management business is, for lack of a better term, a complaint desk, we only get people calling us to complain about something or tell us bad news. Let's face it, it is much like the customer service line you see at the airport when the weather is crappy and there are delays or flight diversions. These are times when people miss their flights or get stuck overnight at the airport. No one in that two-mile line with sleeping bags and fold-out lawn chairs is there to tell that poor customer service representative that they are doing a great job. That's not the time you hear, "I love flying your airline." Pete used to say, "We are the trash men of real estate. No one wants to hang out with us at parties, but they definitely need us." (Not to hurt the feelings of any waste technicians that may be reading this).

Our industry is a systems and procedural-based industry. There are many moving parts.

"Moving parts" means a lot of handoffs between multiple different people, which, as we learned, is necessary when there are processes and procedures that require a variety of roles and departments performing tasks in unison or near unison. When we started, we didn't realize it, but the task of creating these processes, job roles, and departments fell on the shoulders of Pete and me. They do not just appear as the company grows. As you can imagine, this is where problems (or, as our business coach would say, "challenges") show up.

Whenever a task is handed off from one role or department to another, there is a high probability for some things to get overlooked, missed, or miscommunicated to the next person in the chain of tasks. When a company grows at an accelerated pace, the areas that are lacking have a spotlight shone on them. Vulnerabilities light up like a beacon in the night for everyone to see. Empire was no exception. Pete and I discovered that the bigger we grew, the more challenges and choke points we found in our systems. And the bigger they were. Some of them never existed before, they just simply materialized when the business reached a certain maturity, but they were quite evident and caused major stress for our employees.

For instance, using our cell phones to communicate with each other. At one point, we didn't have cell phones.

As the number of properties grew, so did vacant properties that needed to be leased. As we marketed these properties, it caused a lot of phone calls (upwards of one thousand per month). We could not talk on our phones because they would beep non-stop from prospective tenants wanting to know about the properties we had available. On top of that, we had many different types of property owners with different expectations. Five or ten owners is manageable, but eighty to a hundred and our teams would get stressed out. A lot of their time was taken up explaining how we operate. They had to give the same speech over and over again.

We were also upsetting clients, who were leaving us to go to other property management firms because of our non-communication issues and other failures. I will never forget a statistic that shows sixty-eight percent of customers leave a service-based business because they feel the company doesn't care about them anymore. It's not because of price. It's because of ambivalence.

Pete and I realized we had to provide a better and more consistent product to current and future clients if we were going to stay in business. If we did not make pivotal changes and adapt to our growing pains, then we would fall by the wayside like many other entrepreneurs who had great ideas but no backend structure. We would crumble like a house of cards.

Creating Workflows and Streamlining Processes

Knowing that we needed to make this our main focus, we sought out and hired Errol Allen of EA Consulting to help us deliver a better and more consistent product.He came referred to us by our business coach If he could tell us how to provide a better product, then our problems would be solved. Like a genie snapping his fingers, it would be fixed and we could keep the crank of momentum turning. Of course, that is not how these things work. Empire was certainly no exception to the rule, and we found that out through our rigorous education process.

Our whole team sat down with Errol, and the first thing out of his mouth was, "Tell me what you do." It seemed like an easy question, but we bumbled it. When we finally came up with a statement that we agreed on, he asked, "And how do you deliver that?" That hit upon the meat and potatoes of our whole operation, or lack thereof.

Every one of our team members in the room was one hundred percent sure of the answer. The problem was that all of us had a completely different answer. If I was consulting a business, that would be a big red flag. Of course, we were no exception to the many other companies Errol had helped before us. As I look back, I think part of the education process was for Pete and me to hear from our own mouths just how out of sync we were with each other and the rest of the company.

Errol went on to explain that if Empire did not have a common way of delivering our service, then there was no secret or magic pill that he could give us to provide a better customer service experience. In fact, he said, we would be doomed to repeat the missteps of other companies just like ours. He also explained that our accelerated growth would only cause us to crumble faster because we would soon lose customers quicker than we could acquire them. This made a lot of sense to me, and, at that moment, a light bulb went off in my head. Pete's too.

Empire's management had no consistency, so how could we expect our employees to be consistent? How could we expect them to provide a great customer experience if we weren't all on the same page?

It was not an uncommon problem. In reality, it was the standard way small companies operate. While this did make us feel a little better, we also knew that we needed to fix these issues as soon as possible or we would grow ourselves out of business, and that would suck for our wallets.

I suggested we start using basic paper checklists. That would create a mutual understanding between the parties and eventually create some accountability measure for when handoffs happen. As an airline pilot, I was used to checklists. Having trained on Boeing aircraft for twenty years, I knew how to implement them so they worked. I had also seen many cases when checklists were not used properly and catastrophic events followed. In the airline industry, if a pilot fails to perform all the tasks on his checklist and ends up crashing the plane, it's not likely there will be a chance to clear up any confusion later, post crash.

One common challenge with checklists is that, many times, an engineer puts something on a checklist that makes sense based on his book knowledge but that doesn't make sense to the pilot based on his practical experience. In other words, just because it makes sense to the person behind the desk doesn't mean it's a good idea to put it on the checklist. It's similar to when management tells an employee to perform a task that they've never performed themselves. For these reasons, management should always include the people performing the work when making checklists to ensure they are realistic and accurate.

In the airline industry, checklists keep people alive. For example, if a pilot fails to put the landing gear down when landing a plane, that will lead to a crash and lost lives. Another example is when an engine fails and the pilot tries to shut it down but shuts down the wrong engine. If you only have two engines, you'd better prepare for freefall, or hope you're familiar enough with the aerodynamics of a glider plane.

Before you ask, yes, these things actually do happen. Just having a checklist and marking things off as you go without performing the task is a fatal error, and it happens. Imagine having a checklist for driving your car.

Step 1: take out keys
Step 2: put keys in door
Step 3: open door

The challenge with this is that it might make sense to the engineer because it is logical. But it is not practical, and this kind of checklist will not be followed because everyone knows you have to take out your keys and put them in the door before you can drive your car. It's a no-brainer, and people tend to skip over the no-brainers. The one day that something is missed on the checklist, that's the day when things will go catastrophically wrong.

A user may create a checklist that simply says "Step 1: Drive to work." But that's not adequate either.

Back to the issue at hand. Just to put a quick-fix bandaid on our most pressing issues, Pete and I quickly created paper checklists for the things that were killing us, which was mostly everything.

After that, we set our sights on the task of eating the big bad giant elephant. One bite at a time.

We scheduled painstakingly long meetings with our newest best friend and advisor consultant (yes, we hired him on the spot, just like our coach). We met for three hours at a time two to three times per week.

The first thing we had to do was explain in detail what we did for each procedure. To me, this was amazingly boring, and the worse kind of torture. I felt like a Lion pacing a cage, waiting for a chance to get out of there. But I was part of the reason we were in this mess, so I poured all of my attention into it. What's interesting to note is that Pete really shined in this area. With his IT background, it was right up his alley, and he liked where we were going with it. Our consultant would sit, listen, take notes, and ask detailed questions when we'd try to bullshit our way through something, and would tell us to slow down so we could unpack it to make sure there was nothing hidden or that we might be missing.

The truth is, we had no idea how many tasks did or did not get done. Our consultant would never inject by telling us an idea was good or bad. He simply said, "Tell me what you do and how do you do it." Once we got through the explanation, he would take everything we said, put it into a flow chart, and print it out for all of us to look at. Some of these flow charts took up the whole office length and ran up the walls. He would also ask us if the flow chart was correct, or he'd ask how we thought the process went. If we did not agree on something, he would change the flow chart and reprint it. It was an arduous process.

Afterward, we'd bring in all of the employees, or anyone involved in a certain procedure, and get clarification from them as to whether or not the flow chart was correct. Shockingly, or not, there was a large number of employees who said, "I don't do that," or "I didn't know that was my responsibility." We'd also hear someone ask, "Why do we do this here and then someone else does the same thing there?" We found a lot of redundancies, and many things we thought were being done were not being done at all.

This was killing me with a dull spoon. As you may be able to tell, I'm not the most detail oriented person. I am more of a full-throttle-and-get-shit-done-with-a-massive-amount-of-effort- and-then-have-someone-else-go-back-and-make-it-pretty type of person. But it was telling to see just how unorganized we were. That exercise made it very clear why we were not able to deliver a great customer experience.

The next step in the process was to ask the employees involved in the process one pertinent question: "How do you see this flowing better?" When we asked that question, a large conversation, argument, or all-around venting would ensue. It was interesting how much value our employees added when asked, but they wouldn't offer suggestions on their own. It was almost like a free zone where they could speak their minds without getting in trouble. What is funny is that we always asked them for input, but maybe we didn't ask in a way they felt comfortable enough to answer.

I was glad to have our employees' input and involvement. I'm a big believer in teamwork. Collectively, we could build a much better company than if it was just Pete and me. The key to success is getting that input and making sure employees feel like they are a part of the process and solution. Discounting their voices, thoughts, and opinions would be a sure track to failure.

Our consultant feverishly took notes as we all talked over each other throughout this process. We'd go back and forth over a simple "yes" or "no" decision for hours, and, to me, it was tough to maintain focus for that amount of time. But, again, it was necessary to get Empire to the next level.

Errol explained that he should be able to sit in any role in the company, with no prior knowledge of performing a job or task, and know how to do that job or task based on the work flows we were creating in those meetings. We went back and forth over every detail and "what-if" scenario, then he flowed out the new way of doing things. He'd then bring the whole team in and start the process all over again. It was very painful. While I know it was a necessary process, it was like jamming needles into my eyes.

The whole process took about a year and a half. Finally, after many hours of collaborative work, we had a finished product. Or so we thought.

Stretching the systems

Even though we spent over a year and a half working on perfecting our systems and procedures, Pete and I were also becoming aware that challenges arising from managing two hundred properties are much different than the challenges of managing four hundred properties, and the challenges at five hundred did not even exist for us yet. This is common for first businesses, I am told. We didn't know what was lurking around the corner because we had never been down that street before.

It's like the difference between running the first marathon and the twentieth. As we built more businesses, the initial challenges would become more easily solvable since we'd know they are coming, and could be prepared for what we know will be waiting for us at mile nineteen on the next go-round. Or so we hoped.

As we grew, so did the challenges. The good thing was that we became aware that was going to happen and were on the lookout for those new challenges. When they did arise, our radar was up, and we could pivot to make appropriate changes in response. Our business coach told us that fifty percent of our systems will break, and fifty percent of our employees will experience workplace issues as we grow. The faster we grew, he said, the faster we could expect things to go wrong. Our job as leaders was to see those problems and fix them before it was too late. We were trained to look for a tap on the shoulder.

What came after that tap, if we ignored it, was a two by four smacking us. If we ignored that, then a Mack truck would run us over. In other words, ignored problems become bigger problems. The good news was, since we invested so much time and money into creating a solid foundation and had intricate knowledge of our systems and procedures, we had created a foundation for future revisions to be built upon.

Much like the Microsoft software systems--Windows 95,98, 2000 etc.--nothing is "set it and forget it" in business. If you don't change with the environment and you stop solving issues that get in the way of you meeting your clients' needs, you are the next Beta tape in the VHS versus Beta war.

The Japanese have a term for this. It's called Kaizen.

Kaizen means you always have to tweak or adjust something. It is never finished. Pete and I were happy that we had a baseline to start with as well as some solid basic paper checklists to ensure accountability, along with an understanding about how important these tools really were going to be for our future. At least, some variation of those tools.

A Paper Checklist War

The checklists were working. They were crude, but effective. Pete, having come from the IT world, was not a lover of paper, or waste. He was hell bent on turning our office into a paperless environment. I thought it was funny and ironic because, to this day, he carries a paper notebook around so he can list his daily tasks and make notes throughout the day. The guy who demanded the office be paperless and hated our paper checklists was addicted to the process, but not a subscriber to it himself it seemed.

Just to get a rise out of him, I'd put stacks of paper on his desk to see the expression on his face when he noticed them. Our employees would wallpaper his office with used paper as a joke. He was a good sport about it, I will say, but he had a mission and was focused on it. It was creating and implementing a cloud-based checklist to be used company wide in order to standardize our growth.

To give you some background on checklists, the person using them cannot simply agree to check things off. They have to be engaged and actually look at what they are checking off. In the airline industry, planes crash because people check items off a list without performing the task. It happens all the time. Checklist adherence is taught, re-taught, and taught again continually. Every time a pilot goes through his yearly recurrent simulator training, he will also get checklist recurrency training. It's important because it saves lives.

The double-edged sword with checklists is that you can change a procedure by simply changing the checklist. If everyone is using the checklist and not just going through the motions, there will not be any issues when procedures change. However, if things are being done by rote, when procedures change and an airline employee marks an item on a checklist as completed but didn't actually perform it, that's when we see them on the evening news. A property manager not checking off the proper rent amount will not kill people, but if it is missed too often, it could kill a property management business. Charging fees, collecting rent, paying owners, and evicting tenants all affect the bottom line. These are so basic.

You're probably thinking, how could someone miss something so vital? Why would you need a checklist? The checklist is necessary to keep employees focused on tasks that are vital to the success of the organization, even if human life and death aren't the issue.

Checklist Destiny

We had a friend in the property management industry named Kevin Knight who operates a great company in San Antonio, Texas who created an online version of checklists. This individual was well known and well-respected in the industry. He is a good friend of ours to this day. We found out that he started selling these cloud-based checklists. They were valuable because they could be opened from anywhere in the world and on any device, not just one particular computer. Those checklists were general in nature and not specific to any one company or property management software, which was both good and bad. Since every property management company had a different way of doing things, and used a variety of different systems, apps, and gadgets, it was a benefit that these checklists were not specific to his company. For a fee, he would personalize them to a specific company. Empire wasted no time on that offer. We were shifting out of third gear and grinding into fourth for standardization. Our speed and momentum were building.

After having us as a client, I think Kevin decided it was not a good idea to offer this as an option to future customers. Our service package included a certain number of development block hours in order to fit these checklists to our business model and practices. We used those block hours up very quickly and soon needed more time, which we gladly paid for. Because I had been an airline pilot and knew how checklists worked, and Pete being from the IT world, we soon took up the majority of the developer's time. We asked for so many changes it probably wasn't profitable for him to keep us as clients.

We were moving much faster than the standard property management company. Most property management companies had little to no growth. They were semi-stagnant. Empire, however, were revolutionizing the way business was done in the sector, and we were using the checklist to make that happen. It was our spinal cord.

Of course, as we grew, our checklists needed to be updated frequently, and the only person we could rely on was that developer, a guy named Sal, who knew how to do what we needed done. Kevin finally came to us and said that we were taking up too much of Sal's time and we would have to take our business elsewhere. He told us this in a nice Texan sort of way, of course. As much as he liked us as friends, he was losing money on us. We figured that was coming and respected his request.

Trying to find a developer to build a system that had already been started was not an easy task. We went through five different developers. Some were referred to us and we found some online. Quite a few of them were foreign-based. None of them could give us what we needed in the time frame we wanted. It was similar to the challenge we had in the beginning as we churned through SEO rejects. Eventually, we hired a local company to finish our cloud-based checklist. By this time, we had teams working in the Philippines, in India, and in the United States, so it was a necessary accountability tool. It allowed us to see who was in charge of certain tasks by utilizing certain functions of the checklist and assign tasks to different people at various stages of the process.

What Got Us Here Will Not Get Us There

As Empire grew, we religiously attended our weekly coaching sessions. We did everything we were told to do even if it made us uncomfortable. There were days when we'd walk out feeling two inches tall because we failed to complete a task, and there were other days when we'd leave with a pit in our stomachs because we were told we had to do something we didn't think we could or should do. Still, we pushed forward and did everything we were told to do.

I can remember this like it was yesterday. Pete and I would spend weekends smoking cigars and drinking whiskey. We'd get these ideas we thought were simply amazing. But after the booze and cigar haze wore off and we presented the idea to our coach, he told us, without actually saying it, what a dumb idea it was and our entire weekend was wasted. Our dreams were shattered.

I will admit, we did have some dumb ideas. But not all of them were bad ideas. One brainstorm was to create a maintenance company that Empire could sub work out to. And a variation of that was to create a maintenance company other property management firms could sub work out to. We also considered offering eviction services for other property management companies or properties we didn't manage. But, we realized these ideas were taking our focus away from our core business of managing our client assets and delivering unparalleled customer service. Our business coach affectionately referred to this as "the shiny object syndrome." He told us to focus on what we were doing and stay in our vertical.

That was good advice. We soon realized that our success led to other people approaching us with their business ideas and quests for financial domination. They wanted to share in our success, or ask us to join them in theirs. We'd tell ourselves, "We make cheese pizzas and we have to stay within the cheese pizza business."

That's exactly what we did. We got out of doing maintenance on other people's properties and only performed evictions for the properties that we managed. We focused entirely on managing our clients' investments. This gave us complete, unfiltered focus on becoming the best property management company we could be.

The growth continued and we realized that the business practices that got us to this point would not take us further. We wanted to step into a bigger arena, but that required further personal growth and education. Unfortunately, we had our heads buried in the weeds. Being "hands on" operators, we didn't take the time to learn how to grow the company to its full potential. For that matter, we had no idea what our goal for the company was.

We continually sought out more advanced property management professionals who could help us. By engaging other professionals and asking them questions that others would not ask--such as "How do we get better at property management?" and "How can we work harder to make that happen?"--people began to realize that we were not going away. It was not a fluke that our company was gaining momentum. We were cautioned by our coach very early on not to confuse movement with progress. They don't always match, and that's advice I will never forget.

The Maintenance Yo/Yo

The interesting thing about growing a company for the first time is that everything you encounter along the way is a first. Dealing with efficiency, or, should I say "non-efficiency," was no different. Pete and I were not going to be spared that lesson in our Business 101 Masterclass.

Trying to deliver a quality product to our customers on a consistent basis was proving to be more of a challenge as Empire grew larger. Learning how to streamline and systemize our processes was one of our biggest challenges, especially in the maintenance department.

Performing maintenance in a timely manner, and making sure there was accountability with everyone involved on a consistent basis, was a major challenge. Imagine having three or four different air conditioning vendors, several carpet cleaners, and multiple make-ready teams. Trying to track them all, schedule them, and make sure they didn't overcharge our owners, which happened more often than we care to remember. I think this was due, in part, to the fact that these vendors were just as focused on growing their businesses and becoming profitable as we were, and we all had to fight mounting expenses. Dealing with the vendors we did business with at the time was time consuming, but it was vital to our business.

We decided to bring this part of our business in-house, so we created an Empire maintenance division. One of the main drivers for us in doing this was the ability to control workers' time, and quality of work, so we could deliver a consistent product. We hired a maintenance coordinator along with two maintenance technicians to handle the management, we purchased two company maintenance vans that would be stocked with supplies as well.

The focus of these maintenance technicians was to perform small job repairs that could be done as general maintenance, nothing that required a license and nothing that was too expensive or time consuming. For those larger tasks, we would subcontract them to larger companies that specialized in them. Of course, that posed a new challenge for us.

When you have a maintenance person on staff, you have to pay for liability insurance, their salary, company vehicle and the gas it consumes, and other incidentals. The maintenance coordinator was tasked with coordinating and scheduling the technician projects, which have to be done around the availability of the tenant. Of course, tenants had emergencies, jobs, and many other reasons why their schedules didn't fit ours.

We learned that it's hard to turn a profit with maintenance if it is not done on a large volume scale. We had to ask ourselves if it was becoming a distraction--or, as our coach would say, a "shiny object"--from our core business of managing rental properties. Could we grow the business if we controlled maintenance quality?

The cost to operate the maintenance division was quite large. It became harder as expenses grew to see it as a viable business option.

Even though we had maintenance people we trained to our standards, they had their own minds. Maintenance people with hammers and nails are always looking for walls to drive them into. When you send a maintenance guy to bid on a property, he wants to rebuild the house. They want it "done right," which is good for quality of work. However, investors want the house repaired and flipped for as little cost as possible, and as quickly as possible, in order to generate income revenue. Our maintenance guys believed in delivering the best level of service to our clients, so they were aiming for the highest quality of work. Unfortunately, that cost the client more money. It also meant that it took more time to get the property in "rent ready condition" and ultimately frustrated our clients, causing us to lose their business.

It finally hit us in the face that we were, in fact, looking at shiny objects. When that happened, we realized we were in the property management business, not the maintenance business. Maintenance ended up sidetracking us, taking our attention away from our core business, which, again, was managing investor assets. As much as we wanted it to work, we realized we would not be successful in the maintenance business unless we built a company around that core business function. That would entail organizational charts, roles and responsibilities, and processes and procedures. The way we were doing it, we were losing money simply because it was not our focus it was a side project.

What we were trying to do was "bootstrap" it, which means we did not have investors or outside money to give us cash infusions when we needed it. Rather, we were using our own money to float the business. But we didn't have the luxury of losing huge amounts of money just to stay in business. Our wives wouldn't go for that after the rental home fiasco.

What we were doing was not scalable. We came to the hard conclusion that we needed to stop doing internal maintenance and sub it out to quality vendors we could work with.

The first thing we did was sit down with our vendors and establish a clear set of expectations and guidelines. That included quality of work, timeliness, and pricing. In exchange, they would get all of our business.

The next thing we did was have a tough conversation with our maintenance people to inform them we were shutting down the division. Pete and I were so ingrained in the concepts we learned through our business coach that we sat down with our maintenance team and discussed how we could help them create their own maintenance company by "spinning off" from Empire. They would then become our preferred maintenance vendor, and they could go out and get other business simultaneously. We were handing them a great opportunity.

The great thing about that concept was that they knew the Empire system because we trained them. They knew the quality of work that we expected and could help new vendors achieve success in the same way we helped them. It was a true "pay-it-forward" concept. Those maintenance people became our partners, and that built loyalty to our company. They have expressed that they are forever grateful for the chance we provided them, not just for the immediate business but in helping them change their mindset from immigrant worker to business owner.

Since then, our maintenance partners have grown to working with nine local property management companies in Houston and are top on the list of Empire's preferred vendors because of their work ethic and keen business minds. Pete and I could not be prouder and feel that we have helped them achieve success in both a business and personal level. They still get invited to our company parties, and we always enjoy hearing about their successes.

Portfolio Be Divisional

The one thing we heard from our coach over and over again, and from all of our reading on the subject, is: "What got us here, will not get us there."

Marshall Goldsmith is a business genius who has written a book on that very subject. Its title is actually "What Got You Here Won't Get You There." Interestingly, Marshall is coached by the same man who coaches Pete and myself, Doug Winnie. What this phrase means is, personal and company growth is contingent on self-improvement and continuous learning. Pete and I needed to focus on being better leaders. That meant constantly looking for new ways to grow, be innovative, and diligent in taking action.

Another vital aspect of growth is seeing problems before they become problems. Finding the root of a problem and fixing it is a full-time role for leaders. During high-growth mode, overcoming challenges is more important than ever. It's the difference between driving a car at slow speeds while executing a sharp turn and driving at a very fast speed while making the same sharp turn. Rotating the wheel with the same force and cranking at the same torque means one small miscalculation could be catastrophic. The stakes are higher.

The challenge with growing at that pace, since we had never traveled down that path, was that we had no way of knowing what the challenges were going to be. Those turns in the road and major choke points could smash our windshields like a bolt of lightning. Instead of being a tap on the shoulder or a two-by-four hitting us in the chest, it would feel more like a Mack truck barreling down on us. We learned to identify our challenges more quickly, and once you're exposed to them, you know how to see them coming and respond to them more quickly. The challenges that you may have as a one million company are different than the ones you'll have as ten million dollar company, and you can't know what's going to exist at the twenty million dollar level until you get there.

We were told over and over again that fifty percent of our systems and fifty percent of our people will break while we're in high-growth mode, and it will upset clients on the tenant side as well as on the owner side, employee side, and the vendor side. It was something we would have to accept as a part of our growth. Things will never be perfect. It's like repairing a malfunctioning plane while flying it. Some parts won't fix. You gotta figure shit out and improvise until you land.

Tapping our business coach's brain when we had challenges is to this day the most important ingredient to our success. We still rely heavily on his support and guidance as we continue to grow. He taught us how to listen and be ready when other teachers appear so we would be open and ready to receive their message. As time went on, he introduced us to other mentors and coaches who helped us in other areas of our lives, both business and personal.

For example, the more I wanted to learn how to become a better presenter and speaker, the more I started seeking out mentors and coaches who could help me improve at this craft. As I learned the art of public speaking, I focused on getting my message to more people. I needed to shake some trees. So I went "old school" like I did while trying to land an airline job. I sent my bio to every real estate and business radio show and podcast I could find. I ended up getting some larger industry podcasters willing to have me on their shows. They were intrigued with my story, for two reasons. First, because I grew a company from zero to the mid-four-hundred door range. Secondly, because I was still employed as an airline pilot and had the 9/11 background story. It was intriguing to them and inspiring to their listeners. It had the "if I can do it, you can too" feel to it.

I soon started getting more requests to be on more shows in the local Houston area. That led to my becoming a regular on local business talk radio station AM 1070 The Answer. They liked my take on the local real estate industry and property management fundamentals because I spoke from the viewpoint of an investor. I think they really liked the fact that I had multiple layers of education that included investor education as well as property management education. That coupled with my airline pilot training made for an interesting combination.

Several hosts said they really liked my candor and direct talk, maybe because I was not your typical real estate property manager. Looking at me, you would think I'm a cut out from an episode of the motorcycle gang show Sons of Anarchy. My shaved head, tattoos, and two-hundred-thirty-pound frame doesn't fit the property management mold.

Deep down, I think they really enjoyed my off-the-wall airline pilot stories that people only hear in bars. After the show, they'd ask me for new stories to tell. We'd have a few good laughs, or I'd scare them out of their wits. I have a unique way of being able to talk high-level detail with common sense integration, and people understand what I'm saying.

It wasn't long before I was approached with having my own radio show on that same local business talk station, AM 1070 The Answer. I jumped at the chance. I could have my own platform. With a little persuading, we were able to get our maintenance vendors to become show sponsors. That made it a cost-neutral program for us and allowed our sponsors to reach an audience they would not get in front of otherwise.

The main theme of the show was to educate the average investor on real estate tactics and the real estate investor mindset. Whenever I am speaking with an investor, I explain that anybody can buy a property, but it takes a true investor to succeed in the property investing business. When you own real estate, there is a mindset shift from landlord to investor. A landlord is someone who wants to do everything on their own. An investor has a team and leverages that team for their time and experience. I feel the biggest difference between an investor and a landlord is an investor values and respects their time, a landlord does not. Investors get advice and information and use that to make intelligent decisions. When you buy a rental property as an investment, you own four walls and a roof. Operating that investment as a business in order to generate revenue is what makes the investor successful.

The business must have policies, procedures, and a structure. You have to have a business plan wrapped around all of that and a reason you bought that investment property. Simply buying a property for the sake of buying a property is not a recipe for success. As a matter of fact, it is a recipe for disaster.

I know plenty of people who have bought great deals and didn't know what to do with them. I often tell people, "The rubber meets the road the day after you close on a property. No one ever tells you what to do after you own it, and how to actually make a return."

Many wouldbe real estate investors have ended up losing the property and going bankrupt in the process. When I'd later speak with some of these people to identify what the issues had been, it almost always ended up being because they didn't know to take the time to run it as a business. It is rarely the house that makes an investor fail; it is the business model running inside of that property, or lack of it, that causes an investor to fail.

Having the radio show allowed me a much larger platform to get my message to a wider audience. It also helped brand our company, and it also enabled me to become more of an expert when speaking on subjects. Additionally, I was able to promote events we created for clients. Fifty to sixty percent of our clients that owned rental properties did not live in the local Houston area, and many of them didn't live in the United States, so we had a pretty large international client database. We'd take our radio shows and turn them into podcasts so we could send them out via email and social media, which expanded our reach and credibility. It also opened the door to potential new clients, who found us in cyberspace.

G'DAY MATE

One of the many benefits of being involved with NARPM is that Pete and I got to meet a lot of leading experts in the property management industry. As we got more involved, we learned that Australia was, in many ways, more advanced than the United States in this field. In the U.S., roughly eighteen percent of single-family investment properties are managed by property management companies. The other eighty-two percent are self-managed by the individual investor, or, should I say, landlord. In Australia, however, it's almost the polar opposite. Roughly ninety percent of the properties are managed by property management companies and fewer than ten percent are self-managed. One of the reasons for this is Australia has stricter laws. They have tribunals and very stringent tenant protection rights, which make it almost impossible to self-manage in that country.

For this reason, property management is more evolved, and mature, than in the U.S. I will say that the U.S. is catching up quite rapidly, however. There are quite a few more people from Australia that speak on property management than from the U.S.

When Pete was president of the Houston chapter of NARPM, the organization arranged for Darren Hunter from Australia to speak at one of their events. He is a well regarded speaker across Australia and helps property management companies maximize profits. Since Pete was helping him with his accommodations, I offered to let Darren stay at my house. Being a traveler myself, I know how boring it is to stay in hotels all the time and felt it would be nice to show him a little bit of Texas hospitality while he was here, and to get to know him a bit more. As we spent several days together, I filled him in on what I was doing and how I was trying to get my message across via radio shows, podcasts, and video blogs to educate the average investor on some of the pitfalls of real estate investing. Many investors, myself included, have been snared by these pitfalls. Darren felt that I would be a good speaker and wanted to discuss me doing so in Australia. As you can imagine, I gladly agreed.

He then introduced me to his good friend Deniz Yusuf, who was a well-accomplished business development coach in Australia. Deniz coaches and trains business development managers (BDMs) on the art of negotiating and closing property management deals. After several conversations with him, I decided to have him coach my BDM. We both felt that there were enough similarities between the U.S. and Australia to see if his techniques would work in our context. As we discussed the different facets of our industries and how similar they are, I expressed an interest in expanding my speaking career so that my message could reach more people.

Deniz told me he was going to host his own property management convention in Brisbane, Australia that summer and invited me to speak at that event. I was honored to be able to speak to fellow property managers about what we do in the United States and how we were growing our business so rapidly. It turned out that being from America and having my knowledge in the property management industry was very well received in Australia. I spoke four times at the event, all on different topics. I was the hit of the whole event, they said. To me personally, it was inspiring to connect with fellow industry leaders.

That event opened many more doors for me in the Australian market. I have since returned multiple times and have increased my speaking fee every time. To this day, I continue to speak and work with offices in Australia, and I actually pilot the route from Houston to Australia on the Boeing 787. Not only do I get to speak in Australia, but I get to see friends on layovers. It has worked out to be a great relationship, and the Australian people have been nothing but nice and gracious to me. Several of my Outback friends have come to the U.S. and stayed at my house in Texas. When they do, I give them an inside tour of the Empire offices, along with a little bit of Texan hospitality.

Hola Mexico

Back in Houston, the marketing team continued to attract more opportunities while the sales team did an amazing job of closing and bringing on new client's into the company. Our teams learned the art of target acquisition and focused on finding the right clients while always working to bring the cost to acquire that client down. Our conversion rate increased enough that our operations team couldn't keep up. Everyone was stretched thin. As I explained earlier, a challenge that we didn't know existed was soon coming to the forefront.

Remember the maxim? When a company grows, fifty percent of the people and fifty percent of the systems will break. The speed at which they break is directly related to the speed at which the company grows. We soon had a staffing challenge. We had to figure out the right ratio of staff members to properties in our management portfolio. We also tried to predict when to hire people so we were not short when we needed the help.

As a young business in high growth mode, it's a matter of stretching every dollar to operate as efficiently as possible. Sometimes, the Chicken Little came out in us and we decided not to staff up in order to save on expenses. That had the opposite effect than the one we wanted. It caused more stress on the team who weren't able to deliver a good service, which led to upset clients and staff people quitting. As you can imagine, that was the last thing a company wants in heavy growth mode.

We tried to keep employee costs at thirty to thirty-three percent of total monthly revenue, but we were ticking upwards to fifty percent. That's way too high for any business model. It became a major challenge and we had to figure out a way to bring that cost down without killing our staff. We set out to streamline our systems and do more outsourcing in an attempt to leverage offshore human resources and to lower costs.

At the time, we had a good friend in the San Antonio property management business. His company was about the same size as ours. He was outsourcing some of his business tasks, but not from faraway places like Asia and India. He went to Mexico.

As he explained, it made a lot more sense outsourcing to Mexico because it's in the same time zone as Texas. Also, in Texas, there are a lot of immigrants from Mexico. Talking to someone with a Spanish accent is not as uncommon as speaking to someone from India or the Philippines where the language barriers can be much bigger. If you're speaking with someone with a Spanish accent, you don't necessarily think they are a virtual assistant. They could just be an employee from Mexico.

We were already familiar with using virtual assistants for low-level tasks, but we didn't realize the extent to which they could be utilized. The barriers included language, communication, and time of day. These challenges were eliminated when working with assistants in Mexico. We connected with a company with an outsourcing channel for virtual assistants in Mexico. Once we started talking to these potential employees, we realized how talented they were, and the depth of abilities that they had. Almost instantly, we filled many roles with team members in Mexico.

To this day, it has proven to be a successful business model for us. We not only were able to lower employee expenses, but we also increased productivity. The attention to detail these virtual assistants brought to the table has been a pleasant surprise.

The challenge with using virtual assistants, in any business, is it only works as well as the system created around the role. The job duties must be explained in detail, and you must be able to duplicate it over and over again. If you should need to add or replace team members, you don't have to start from the beginning. This is where we used the online checklists we talked about in the previous chapter, our systems and procedural manuals, and a lot of video knowledge-base library education tools.

This structure has enabled us to add team members with very short training time. We even got to the point where we created virtual assistant team leaders. A part of their job role was teaching new team members how to perform certain tasks per our company policy. We believed we had a way to scale our business model and expand it beyond Houston to other cities.

We were so committed to using the team members in Mexico that we went to the company that contracted them and negotiated a deal to buy them out of the contract. This process started when our team members approached us and asked to join the company as employees. They believed so much in our culture and our brand that they clearly stated they wanted to have the security of working directly for us.

When working for a contract company, we learned, the contract company could, at any time, pull that person and place them with another company. While this is not likely to happen, it is a possibility. These contract workers wanted job security for themselves and their families. We were able to provide it for them, and I'm happy to say that all of the contract workers were excited about the move and became a part of the Empire team.

Time to Stretch Houston

Houston being the fourth largest metropolitan city in the United States means it is also one of the biggest in geographical areas. It can take a long time to drive from one end of Houston to the other. It can take as long as two-and-a-half to three hours in some traffic conditions. A sales person on the south side of town needing to travel to a sales call on the northern side of Houston where our property management company is located can present a time and productivity challenge. My sales people were running into a lot of windshield time, which caused us to lose deals because they couldn't get to the clients fast enough.

We also solicited the help of a new business partner, Brad Sugars, who was the founder of ActionCOACH, the company that had been coaching us from inception. We brought him on board to help us grow across the United States in either a franchising, licensing, or business acquisition model. We realized that we had to ensure we could stretch our business model, scale it, and easily duplicate it. In order for this to happen in other cities, the first task was to expand the model in Houston. We took our business model and broke it down to match the city sectors. We put small off-satellite offices throughout the city to expand our business footprint. That included small divisional sectors and business developers in each sector so the geographic areas of our business were smaller and more manageable. These divisions would operate like mini-teams and included a property manager, BDM, and a few real estate agents in each office. It would all be backed up by virtual assistants in Mexico. That was the first phase in our growth process allowing us to test our systems before we expanding into the next city.

Attacking Big DFW

Shortly after stretching Houston, then making some tweaks and minor adjustments, we realized we were ready to move into the next city. We set our eyes on the Dallas-Fort Worth area. Since that market is comparable to the Houston market, with similar property management clients and fee structures, as well as having similar investors, it made sense and was close enough to drive to.

The DFW Metroplex was going to be our beta test so that when we decided to license our model we could show that our business can go into a new city without any market share or anyone knowing who we were, open offices, and, in a short time, become the property management company of choice. This was a big step for us because we had to test our systems to see if they could be duplicated in another city, and to see if our model was scalable. We also had to make sure our standardization practices worked.

As of this writing, we are operating in Dallas-Fort Worth. We have one office in Dallas and one in Fort Worth. We are making a name for ourselves in that market with radio shows, local charities involving war veterans, public speaking, sponsoring events, and teaching real estate classes. Most importantly, we are now actually managing properties in both of those cities.

We have proven that our business model works. Now, our eyes are set to grow in multiple cities and start the licensing model to sell to other people around the country. The last piece of the puzzle is finding great talent in each city we are planning to expand into. Since real estate is a fluid and dynamic industry with so many variables, it's hard to make sure you have the right person in the right seat when you may be five hundred to over one thousand miles away. This posed a major challenge to us for growth and scalability. Being able to deliver the same level of service on a consistent basis was a must in order for us to expand.

Tier 1 Communication Centers

Our biggest challenge has been systems continuity. Going back to what we learned from Errol when we decided to eat this elephant, the more handoffs involved increases chances that something will be missed. Our property managers continued to be stressed and maxed out on time. Even though we continuously found tasks to offload to our team in Mexico, along with using technology to streamline things, the team was constantly missing things and upsetting clients. In order to de-stress the staff, we would let them work from home thinking it didn't matter where they were working as long as their weekly key performance indicators came in where we needed them to be.

However, when customer complaints came in, due to lack of communication and follow up, the issue hit our radar. When we started losing clients, we had a bigger problem. As I explained earlier, this starts as a tap on the shoulder, which is followed by a two-by-four hitting you over the head. Finally, a Mack truck runs you over. This is the hierarchy of problems as they grow in size, and if you choose to not deal with them when they arise, you'll reap the consequences.

Our director of property operations, Margo, was spending eighty percent of her time on an apology tour trying to put out fires. Her chief responsibility became persuading property owners to not walk out the door. It was clear that we had a Mack truck coming through the front door.

Just to give a time reference, this was two months after we realized we may have an operations issue. The lesson here is that problems can escalate very quickly if not addressed. It started as a tap on the shoulder and quickly escalated to the Mack truck.

Again, Pete's and my job was to see the issues coming and find solutions as quickly as we could. One question we got in the habit of asking ourselves was, "Is this a system problem or a people problem?" This one was a combination of both, but, often, one causes the other. Which one, you may ask, do you fix first? That is up for interpretation. We learned that when you have a problem you need to look upstream at what is causing the problem. If you just focus on how to address the problem and deal with issues as they arise, you become a reactionary company and never fix the reason why your problems are happening.

We knew we had to change things quickly in order to change our direction, and that is exactly what we did.

The first thing we did was bring the property managers back into the office. No more working at home. We considered working from home was a privilege, not a right. We knew our property managers and teams worked hard and believed in our core values, so that was not the issue. Many of them worked before and after their scheduled hours to provide the best service they could to our clients. Our focus was getting our customers the service we promised them and to earn their trust so that they could feel confident in us managing their investments, which numbered in the hundreds of thousands of dollars. Investment properties are typically the second largest investment people have, right next to their personal homes.

While we were creating our work-at-home policy, we realized a way to scale our business yet again was through leveraging more teams and outsourcing more tasks.

We came to realize that this type of challenge is common in the property management business. In any business there are multiple handoffs. There are procedures and a need for strict standardization. There are also many stress points and growing pains. Finding scalable solutions was not just a problem for Empire. It's a Business 101 problem. Okay, maybe it's Business 202, but you get my point.

Even though we had checklists that were specific to our operations, cloud-based, and with built-in abilities to set up take-action notices for the next individual in the handoff chain, the process wasn't working the way we wanted it to. I'm still not sure if the challenge was too many expectations on the in-house team or if it was the wrong person in the wrong seat of the bus. It may have been a combination, but this was not an issue that was going to stop us or slow us down.

To solve these challenges, we decided to take a look at the issues from another perspective. Instead of being harder on the in-house team, who clearly were trying to do the best they could, we considered offloading some responsibility so they could focus on their primary jobs. We took our team members from Mexico and turned them into team centers with very specific roles and tasks. Like the old saying goes, 'What gets measured, gets improved."

Within a month of creating these divisions, customer complaints went down. Communication effectiveness from Empire to our clients went up along with customer satisfaction.

As we continued to grow our company, we added team members to the centers. The team members all worked together inside of their respective team centers, and since they were focused on very specific tasks and goals, it was much easier to train them to achieve the necessary accomplishments. "Less is more" truly became a realization.

The key to our success was to first have the right people doing the right job, having clear accountability procedures, and a way to measure accountability with weekly key performance indicators. The system worked. Our goal was to take the load off the in-house teams so they could perform their tasks, such as walk properties, execute move-in and move-out inspections, handle court evictions, provide good customer service, etc. We wanted to call our customers not just when bad news needed to be communicated, but also just to check in on them so we could create positive customer experiences. We called those "feel good calls." Other time consuming things that could be offloaded were handed to another team.

Conclusion

We are now finishing out the proof of concept for our expansion and continuing our multiple city growth plan. Unknown to my partner Pete Neubig or myself, this wild ride would take us on a journey that was beyond our wildest imaginations without knowing where it will take us in the future.

Our goal to create a one hundred million dollar company was created on the tragic day of 9/11. That day indirectly changed the course of my life forever. Unknown to my partner Pete Neubig or myself, where this wild ride would take us when we began this journey was beyond our imaginations. Not knowing where the turns, pitfalls, or other ugly hairy monsters lurked proved to be an unforgettable adventure. But the one thing we did do is take action. Whether it was right action or wrong action, it was, without a doubt, consistent and massive.

See you out there on the battlefield of business. I hope my story has entertained and more importantly inspired you and helped educate you on some key property management practices. Thank you again for your time. I was told "You can always make more money, but you can never make more time." The fact that you invested your time with me while reading this book means the world to me.

As we say in flying: "Keep the blue side up and always have a tailwind."

CPSIA information can be obtained
at www.ICGtesting.com
Printed in the USA
LVHW110748210420
654167LV00001B/325

9 781095 026731